BORDEN

Recipe Collection

BEEKMAN HOUSE
New York

CONTENTS

Microwave Cooking
Microwave ovens vary in wattage and power output; cooking times given with microwave directions in this book may need to be adjusted.

©1986, 1987 Borden, Inc.

Some Borden products are in limited distribution.

Recipe Development:
  Borden Kitchens
  Annie Watts Cloncs, Director

Photography Coordination:
Mallard Marketing Associates, Inc.

Library of Congress Catalog Card Number: 86-60771

ISBN: 0-517-61931-8

This edition published by:
Beekman House
Distributed by Crown Publishers, Inc.

Pictured on front cover: *Baked Ham with Tangy Coconut Ham Glaze* (see page 33), *Tossed Salad with Lemon Vinaigrette Dressing* (see page 28), *Golden Cauliflower Soup* (see page 15), *Cherry Cheese Pie* (see page 67) and *Southern Sunshine* (see page 20).

Pictured on back cover: *Stir-Fried Beef and Vegetables* (see page 47), *Moist Orange Mince Muffins* and *Chocolate Spice Surprise Muffins* (see page 57), *Layered Taco Dip* (see page 5) and *Crumbly-Topped Lemon Mince Bars* and *Chocolate Fruit Truffles* (see pages 84 and 85).

Printed and bound by Tiskarna Slovenija, Yugoslavia
j i h g f e d c b

Borden is pleased to present this collection of more than 200 recipes featuring many of our food products! For more than 130 years, Borden has been providing American consumers with high quality foods developed to meet ever-changing lifestyles and cooking trends.

In 1857, with three employees and one product, Gail Borden founded the company that has become Borden, Inc., a leading international manufacturer of food and dairy products.

That first product, Eagle® Brand Sweetened Condensed Milk, is still among the diverse line of items marketed by Borden. In 1885, Borden's expansion began when fresh milk was added to its product line. In the 1920's, ice cream and cheese furthered Borden's interest in dairy foods. In the 30's, Elsie, the beloved spokescow for Borden dairy products, was created. Today, Borden milk and ice cream are the most widely distributed brand of dairy products in the U.S.A.

A 60's expansion program brought many well-known food brands into the Borden family: ReaLemon® and ReaLime® Juices from Concentrate; Wyler's® Bouillons; those traditional New England favorites—Snow's® Chowders and Clams; Bama® Jams and Jellies—the most popular brand of jellies in the South; Campfire® Marshmallows; and everyone's favorite confection, Cracker Jack® Caramel Coated Popcorn and Peanuts; as well as Wise® snack products, the leading selling brand of potato chips on the East coast.

Other widely known Borden brands include None Such® Mincemeat—a holiday tradition for more than a century, Kava® Instant Coffee, Cremora® Non-Dairy Creamer, Coco Lopez® Cream of Coconut—the original ingredient used to create the pina colada, and Line-line® cheese products, the most popular brand in the diet cheese category.

In the 1970's and 80's, Borden's growth has been in the pasta, specialty grocery, snack food and dairy lines with the acquisition of several quality brands. Creamette is the flagship brand in the Borden pasta family, along with regional brands—Anthony's, Bravo, Gioia, Globe A-1, Luxury, Merlino's, Mrs. Grass, New Mill, Pennsylvania Dutch, R&F, Red Cross, Ronco and Vimco. Meadow Gold® and Viva® dairy products were acquired by Borden. Wise® snacks have been joined by popular regional brands—Guy's, Buckeye, Geiser's, La Famous, Clover Club, Jays and Seyfert's.

The first recipes using Borden's original product, Eagle® Brand Sweetened Condensed Milk, were published more than a century ago. Then, as now, consumers were looking for high quality, family-pleasing foods that were convenient and easy to prepare.

Since the 1920's, the Borden Kitchens have been developing recipes using Borden products. The recipes in the BORDEN RECIPE COLLECTION were developed and tested by the home economists of the Borden Kitchens to ensure the easy preparation, good taste and high quality that generations of American cooks from coast to coast have come to expect from Borden. Enjoy!

APPETIZERS & SOUPS

Looking for that perfect party food or delicious meal starter? Select from a bounty of tantalizing soups—light to hearty. Or serve a quick dip or creamy spread with crunchy fresh vegetables or crisp chips. For that special touch, create a tasty tidbit like stuffed shrimp, Tropical Sausage Bites or Teriyaki Wing Dings.

◄LAYERED TACO DIP

Makes 12 to 15 servings

1 pound lean ground beef
1 (4-ounce) can chopped green chilies, undrained
2 teaspoons Wyler's® Beef-Flavor Instant Bouillon
1 (16-ounce) container Borden® Sour Cream
1 (1⅛-ounce) package taco seasoning mix
1 (16-ounce) can refried beans
1 (6-ounce) container frozen avocado dip, thawed
Shredded cheese, chopped tomatoes, sliced green onions, sliced ripe olives
Wise® Bravos® or La Famous® Tortilla Chips

In large skillet, brown meat; pour off fat. Add chilies and bouillon; cook and stir until bouillon dissolves. Cool. In small bowl, combine sour cream and taco seasoning mix; set aside. In 7- *or* 8-inch springform pan or on large plate, spread beans. Top with meat mixture, sour cream mixture and avocado dip. Cover and chill several hours. Just before serving, garnish with cheese, tomatoes, onions and olives. Serve with tortilla chips. Refrigerate leftovers.

SWEET 'N' SOUR MEATBALLS

Makes about 5 dozen

1½ pounds lean ground beef
1 (8-ounce) can water chestnuts, drained and chopped
2 eggs
⅓ cup dry bread crumbs
1 tablespoon Worcestershire sauce
4 teaspoons Wyler's® Beef-Flavor Instant Bouillon
1 cup water
½ cup firmly packed light brown sugar
½ cup ReaLemon® Lemon Juice from Concentrate
¼ cup catsup
2 tablespoons cornstarch
¼ teaspoon salt
1 large red or green pepper, cut into squares
Chopped parsley, optional

In large bowl, combine meat, water chestnuts, eggs, bread crumbs, Worcestershire and bouillon; mix well. Shape into 1¼-inch meatballs. In large skillet, brown meatballs. Remove from pan; pour off fat. In skillet, combine remaining ingredients except pepper and parsley; mix well. Over medium heat, cook and stir until sauce thickens. Reduce heat. Add meatballs; simmer uncovered 10 minutes. Add pepper; heat through. Garnish with parsley if desired. Refrigerate leftovers.

BLUSHING ONION SOUP

Makes eight 1-cup servings

4 cups thinly sliced onions
1 clove garlic, finely chopped
¼ cup margarine or butter
1 (46-ounce) can tomato juice
1 cup water
2 teaspoons Wyler's® Beef-Flavor
    Instant Bouillon *or* 2 Beef-Flavor
    Bouillon Cubes
2 teaspoons parsley flakes
8 slices French bread, toasted
2 cups (8 ounces) shredded Mozzarella
    cheese

In large kettle or Dutch oven, cook onions and garlic in margarine until tender. Stir in tomato juice, water, bouillon and parsley. Bring to a boil; reduce heat. Simmer uncovered 20 to 30 minutes; stir occasionally. Ladle into 8 oven-proof soup bowls. Top with bread slices and sprinkle generously with cheese. Broil 2 to 3 minutes or until cheese melts. Serve immediately.

MICROWAVE: In 2-quart glass measure, melt margarine on 100% power (high) 1 minute. Add onions and garlic; cook covered on 100% power (high) 5 to 6 minutes or until onions are tender, stirring after 2 minutes. Add tomato juice, water, bouillon and parsley. Cook covered on 100% power (high) 15 to 17 minutes or until boiling. Proceed as above.

Blushing Onion Soup

HOT SPINACH DIP   ▲

Makes about 2 cups

1 (10-ounce) package frozen chopped
    spinach, thawed and well drained
1 (8-ounce) package cream cheese,
    softened
½ cup Borden® Milk
2 tablespoons margarine or butter
2 teaspoons Wyler's® Chicken-Flavor
    Instant Bouillon
⅛ teaspoon ground nutmeg
1 tablespoon ReaLemon® Lemon Juice
    from Concentrate
    Melba rounds

In medium saucepan, combine cheese, milk, margarine, bouillon and nutmeg. Over low heat, cook and stir until thickened and smooth. Stir in spinach; heat through. Remove from heat; add ReaLemon. Serve hot in chafing dish with Melba rounds. Refrigerate leftovers.

MICROWAVE: In 1-quart glass measure, cook cheese, milk, margarine, bouillon and nutmeg on 50% power (medium) 5 to 6 minutes, stirring every 2 minutes. Stir in spinach; cook on 50% power (medium) 2 to 3 minutes or until hot. Proceed as above.

TROPICAL SAUSAGE BITES ▶

Makes about 40 appetizer servings

1½ pounds smoked sausage, cut into
    ½-inch pieces
1 tablespoon margarine or butter
2 tablespoons cornstarch
1 (20-ounce) can juice-packed
    pineapple chunks, drained,
    reserving juice
½ cup Coco Lopez® Cream of Coconut
2 tablespoons prepared mustard
¼ teaspoon garlic powder
1 large green or red pepper, cut into
    1-inch pieces
1 (8-ounce) can water chestnuts,
    drained and halved

In large skillet, brown sausage in margarine; pour off fat. In small bowl, stir together cornstarch, reserved pineapple juice, cream of coconut, mustard and garlic powder; add to sausage in skillet. Cook and stir until sauce thickens. Add pineapple, pepper and water chestnuts; heat through. Refrigerate leftovers.

MICROWAVE: In 12 × 7-inch baking dish, combine sausage and margarine; cover with wax paper. Cook on 100% power (high) 5 minutes, stirring after 2½ minutes; pour off fat. In 1-quart glass measure, combine cornstarch, reserved pineapple juice, cream of coconut, mustard and garlic powder; mix well. Cook on 100% power (high) 3 to 3½ minutes or until thick, stirring after 2 minutes. Pour sauce over sausage; stir in pineapple, pepper and water chestnuts. Cook on 100% power (high) 3 to 4 minutes or until heated through.

CLAM CHEESE BALL

Makes one 3-inch cheese ball

1 (8-ounce) package cream cheese,
    softened
1 (6½-ounce) can Snow's® or Doxsee
    Minced Clams, well drained
½ teaspoon cracked pepper
½ teaspoon onion salt
¼ cup grated Parmesan cheese
1 tablespoon chopped parsley
    Melba rounds

In small mixer bowl, beat cream cheese until fluffy. Stir in clams, pepper and onion salt. Chill about 1 hour. Shape into ball. Combine Parmesan cheese and parsley; roll ball in cheese mixture. Chill 1 hour. Serve with Melba rounds. Refrigerate leftovers.

MANHATTAN CLAM DIP

Makes about 1⅔ cups

1 (8-ounce) container Borden® Sour
    Cream
¼ cup Bennett's® Chili Sauce
1 (6½-ounce) can Snow's® or Doxsee
    Minced Clams, drained
¼ cup mayonnaise or salad dressing
1 tablespoon finely chopped green
    onion
1 teaspoon ReaLemon® Lemon Juice
    from Concentrate

In small bowl, combine ingredients; mix well. Chill before serving. Garnish as desired. Serve with Wise® Cottage Fries® Potato Chips or assorted vegetables. Refrigerate leftovers.

Hearty Vegetable Soup

MARINATED MUSHROOMS

Makes about 3 cups

½ cup vegetable oil
⅓ cup ReaLemon® Lemon Juice from
　　Concentrate
¼ cup water
3 to 4 teaspoons sugar
1 teaspoon garlic salt
1 teaspoon thyme leaves
1 pound small whole fresh mushrooms,
　　cleaned

In medium saucepan, combine all ingredients
except mushrooms; bring to a boil. Add
mushrooms; reduce heat. Simmer uncovered
10 minutes. Cover; refrigerate overnight to
blend flavors.

SPINACH VEGETABLE DIP

Makes about 4 cups

1 (16-ounce) container Borden® Sour
　　Cream
1 (10-ounce) package frozen chopped
　　spinach, thawed and drained
1 (1.7-ounce) package Mrs. Grass®
　　Homestyle Vegetable Dip and
　　Soup Mix
2 tablespoons Borden® Milk
Melba rounds

In medium bowl, combine sour cream, spinach,
dip mix and milk; mix well. Chill 3 hours to
blend flavors. Stir before serving. Serve with
Melba rounds. Refrigerate leftovers.

HEARTY VEGETABLE SOUP

Makes about 3 quarts

3 pounds beef shanks, cracked
8 cups water
3 tablespoons Wyler's® Beef-Flavor
　　Instant Bouillon *or* 9 Beef-Flavor
　　Bouillon Cubes
2 bay leaves
1 (28-ounce) can whole tomatoes,
　　undrained
1 cup pared, sliced carrots
½ cup chopped celery
½ cup chopped onion
1 teaspoon thyme leaves
1 cup uncooked Creamettes® Elbow
　　Macaroni
2 cups sliced zucchini (2 small)

In large kettle or Dutch oven, combine shanks,
water, bouillon and bay leaves. Bring to a boil;
simmer covered 1½ hours or until meat is
tender. Remove shanks and bay leaves; cut
meat into cubes. Discard bones. Cool stock;
skim fat from surface. Add meat, tomatoes,
carrots, celery, onion and thyme; simmer
covered 20 minutes. Add macaroni and
zucchini. Cook 10 minutes longer or until
tender. Refrigerate leftovers.

SAVORY STUFFED MUSHROOMS

Makes 18 to 24 appetizers

4 slices bacon, cooked and crumbled, reserving 2 tablespoons drippings
¼ cup chopped onion
1 clove garlic, finely chopped
1 cup Borden® Cottage Cheese
1 teaspoon Wyler's® Chicken-Flavor Instant Bouillon
1 cup herb-seasoned stuffing mix
18 to 24 large fresh mushroom caps
Melted margarine
Pimiento strips

Preheat oven to 350°. In small skillet, cook onion and garlic in reserved drippings until tender. In medium bowl, combine all ingredients except mushrooms, melted margarine and pimiento. Brush mushrooms with melted margarine; fill with stuffing mixture, mounding slightly. Garnish with pimiento. Place in shallow baking dish; bake 10 to 12 minutes. Serve hot. Refrigerate leftovers.

MICROWAVE: In 1-quart glass measure, combine drippings, onion and garlic. Cook on 100% power (high) 1 minute. Proceed as above. Arrange half of mushrooms on large round microwave-safe plate. Cook on 100% power (high) 3 to 5 minutes, rotating plate once during cooking. Repeat with remaining mushrooms.

CREAMY TOMATO BISQUE

Makes about 2½ quarts

2 cups water
1 (14½-ounce) can tomatoes, undrained
½ cup chopped celery
2 tablespoons chopped onion
5 teaspoons Wyler's® Chicken-Flavor Instant Bouillon or 5 Chicken-Flavor Bouillon Cubes
2 medium tomatoes, pared and diced
¼ cup margarine or butter
3 tablespoons flour
2 cups (1 pint) Borden® Coffee Cream or Half-and-Half
1 tablespoon sugar

In large saucepan, combine water, canned tomatoes, celery, onion and bouillon; cover and simmer 20 minutes. Place in blender container; blend until smooth. In same pan, cook fresh tomatoes in *2 tablespoons* margarine about 5 minutes; remove from pan. In same pan, melt remaining *2 tablespoons* margarine; stir in flour. Add cream; over low heat, cook and stir until thickened. Stir in bouillon mixture, tomatoes and sugar; heat through (*do not boil*). Garnish as desired. Refrigerate leftovers.

NUTTY BLUE CHEESE VEGETABLE DIP

Makes about 2 cups

1 cup mayonnaise or salad dressing
1 (8-ounce) container Borden® Sour Cream
¼ cup (1 ounce) crumbled blue cheese
1 tablespoon finely chopped onion
2 teaspoons Wyler's® Beef-Flavor Instant Bouillon
½ to ¾ cup coarsely chopped walnuts
Assorted fresh vegetables

In medium bowl, combine mayonnaise, sour cream, blue cheese, onion and bouillon; mix well. Stir in nuts; cover and chill. Stir before serving. Garnish as desired. Serve with vegetables. Refrigerate leftovers.

Nutty Blue Cheese Vegetable Dip

MINI MEAT PIES

Makes about 40 appetizers

½ **pound lean ground beef, browned and drained**
2 **hard-cooked eggs, finely chopped**
¼ **cup Borden® Sour Cream**
1 **tablespoon chopped parsley**
1 **teaspoon Wyler's® Beef-Flavor Instant Bouillon**
1 **(11-ounce) package pie crust mix**

Preheat oven to 400°. In medium bowl, combine all ingredients except pie crust mix; mix well. Prepare pie crust mix as package directs. Divide dough in half. On floured surface, roll out half the dough to 10×13-inch rectangle, ⅛-inch thick; cut into twenty 2½-inch squares. Spoon 1 heaping teaspoon meat mixture in center of each square; fold as desired. Repeat with remaining dough and meat mixture. Place 1 inch apart on ungreased baking sheets. Bake 12 to 15 minutes or until lightly browned. Serve hot. Refrigerate leftovers.

TERIYAKI WING DINGS ▲

Makes about 3 dozen

⅓ **cup ReaLemon® Lemon Juice from Concentrate**
¼ **cup catsup**
¼ **cup soy sauce**
¼ **cup vegetable oil**
2 **tablespoons brown sugar**
¼ **teaspoon garlic powder**
¼ **teaspoon pepper**
3 **pounds chicken wing drumettes *or* chicken wings, cut at joints and wing tips removed**

To make teriyaki marinade, combine all ingredients except chicken; mix well. Place chicken in shallow baking dish; pour marinade over. Cover; refrigerate 6 hours or overnight, turning occasionally. Preheat oven to 375°. Arrange chicken on rack in aluminum foil-lined shallow baking pan. Bake 40 to 45 minutes, basting occasionally with marinade. Refrigerate leftovers.

MICROWAVE: Marinate chicken as above. Divide chicken and marinade between two 8-inch baking dishes. Cover with wax paper; cook each dish on 100% power (high) 12 to 14 minutes or until tender, rearranging pieces once or twice.

CALICO CLAM SPREAD

Makes about 2 cups

1 **(8-ounce) package cream cheese, softened**
1 **tablespoon ReaLemon® Lemon Juice from Concentrate**
1 **teaspoon prepared mustard**
1 **teaspoon Worcestershire sauce**
2 **(6½-ounce) cans Snow's® or Doxsee Chopped Clams, drained**
⅓ **cup finely crushed saltine cracker crumbs (about 8 crackers)**
1 **(2-ounce) jar sliced pimientos, drained and chopped**
2 **tablespoons finely chopped onion**
2 **tablespoons chopped parsley**
   Melba rounds

In small mixer bowl, beat cheese, ReaLemon, mustard and Worcestershire until fluffy. Stir in clams, crumbs, pimientos, onion and parsley; mix well. Chill 2 to 3 hours to blend flavors. Serve with Melba rounds. Refrigerate leftovers.

STUFFED EGGS

Makes 24 appetizers

12 hard-cooked eggs, shelled and halved
½ cup salad dressing or mayonnaise
1 tablespoon Borden® Milk
1 tablespoon cider vinegar
1 teaspoon Wyler's® Chicken-Flavor Instant Bouillon
1 teaspoon prepared mustard
1 teaspoon sugar
Sliced pimiento-stuffed olives

Remove yolks from whites. In small mixer bowl, combine yolks and remaining ingredients except olives; beat until smooth. Spoon or pipe into egg whites. Garnish with olives. Chill. Refrigerate leftovers.

QUICK PATÉ MOLD

Makes 1 appetizer mold

½ pound liverwurst, cut into small pieces
1 (8-ounce) package cream cheese, softened
2 tablespoons finely chopped onion
1 teaspoon Wyler's® Chicken-Flavor Instant Bouillon
Parsley, optional
Melba rounds

In small mixer bowl, combine liverwurst, cheese, onion and bouillon; beat until smooth. Turn into well-oiled 2-cup mold. Chill. Unmold; garnish with parsley if desired. Serve with Melba rounds. Refrigerate leftovers.

HOT SAUSAGE BITES

Makes about 3 dozen

½ pound bulk sausage, browned and drained
1½ cups biscuit baking mix
1 cup (4 ounces) shredded mild Cheddar cheese
⅓ cup water
1 teaspoon Wyler's® Beef-Flavor Instant Bouillon

Preheat oven to 400°. In medium bowl, combine ingredients; mix well. Shape into small balls. Place 1 inch apart on lightly greased baking sheets. Bake 12 to 15 minutes or until edges are lightly browned. Remove from baking sheets immediately. Serve hot. Refrigerate leftovers.

VEGETABLE TUNA DIP

Makes about 4 cups

1 cup mayonnaise or salad dressing
1 (8-ounce) container Borden® Sour Cream
1 (6½-ounce) can tuna, drained
1 (1.7-ounce) package Mrs. Grass® Homestyle Vegetable Dip and Soup Mix
2 tablespoons ReaLemon® Lemon Juice from Concentrate
1 teaspoon prepared horseradish, optional

In medium bowl, combine ingredients; mix well. Chill 3 hours to blend flavors. Stir before serving. Serve with fresh vegetables or potato chips. Refrigerate leftovers.

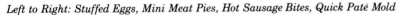

Left to Right: Stuffed Eggs, Mini Meat Pies, Hot Sausage Bites, Quick Paté Mold

WARM HERB CHEESE SPREAD ▲

Makes about 4 cups

3 (8-ounce) packages cream cheese,
    softened
¼ cup Borden® Milk
¼ cup ReaLemon® Lemon Juice from
    Concentrate
½ teaspoon *each* basil, marjoram,
    oregano and thyme leaves
¼ teaspoon garlic powder
½ pound cooked shrimp, chopped
    (1½ cups), optional

Preheat oven to 350°. In large mixer bowl, beat
cheese *just* until smooth. Gradually beat in
milk then ReaLemon. Stir in remaining
ingredients. Pour into 8- or 9-inch quiche dish
or pie plate. Cover; bake 15 minutes or until
hot. Garnish as desired. Serve warm with
assorted crackers or vegetables. Refrigerate
leftovers.

MICROWAVE: Prepare cheese spread as
above; pour into 8- or 9-inch glass pie plate.
Heat on 50% power (medium) 5 to 6 minutes
or until hot. Stir before serving.

TERIYAKI SCALLOP ROLL-UPS

Makes about 2 dozen

12 slices bacon, partially cooked and cut
    in half crosswise
⅓ cup ReaLime® Lime Juice from
    Concentrate
¼ cup soy sauce
¼ cup vegetable oil
1 tablespoon light brown sugar
2 cloves garlic, finely chopped
½ teaspoon pepper
½ pound sea scallops, cut in half
24 fresh pea pods
12 water chestnuts, cut in half

To make teriyaki marinade, combine ReaLime,
soy sauce, oil, sugar, garlic and pepper; mix
well. Wrap 1 scallop half, 1 pea pod and 1
water chestnut half in each bacon slice; secure
with wooden pick. Place in shallow baking
dish; pour marinade over. Cover; refrigerate 4
hours or overnight, stirring occasionally.
Preheat oven to 450°. Place roll-ups on rack in
aluminum foil-lined shallow baking pan; bake
6 minutes. Turn; continue baking 6 minutes or
until bacon is crisp. Serve hot. Refrigerate
leftovers.

BAKED STUFFED SHRIMP ▶

Makes 6 to 8 servings

1 pound jumbo raw shrimp (about 12 to 16), peeled, leaving tails on
1 cup chopped mushrooms
⅓ cup chopped onion
1 clove garlic, finely chopped
1 teaspoon Wyler's® Chicken-Flavor Instant Bouillon
¼ cup margarine or butter
1½ cups soft bread crumbs (3 slices bread)
1 tablespoon chopped pimiento
Melted margarine or butter
Chopped parsley, optional

Preheat oven to 400°. In large skillet, cook mushrooms, onion, garlic and bouillon in margarine until tender. Remove from heat; stir in crumbs and pimiento. Cut a slit along underside of each shrimp; do not cut through. Remove vein; brush entire shrimp with margarine. Mound stuffing mixture in hollow of each shrimp. Place in greased shallow baking dish. Bake 10 to 12 minutes or until hot. Garnish with parsley if desired. Refrigerate leftovers.

MICROWAVE: In 1-quart glass measure, melt margarine on 100% power (high) 45 seconds. Add mushrooms, onion, garlic and bouillon. Cook on 100% power (high) 3 minutes or until onion is tender. Stir in crumbs and pimiento. Prepare shrimp as above. Place in two greased 12 × 7-inch baking dishes or one (12-inch) round glass platter. Cook on 100% power (high) 3 minutes or until hot. Proceed as above.

SWEET & SOUR GLAZE

Makes about 2 cups

1 cup Bama® Apricot or Peach Preserves
1 (8-ounce) bottle Russian salad dressing
1 tablespoon Wyler's® Beef-Flavor Instant Bouillon or 3 Beef-Flavor Bouillon Cubes
½ cup finely chopped onion
1 clove garlic, chopped

In medium saucepan, combine ingredients; cook and stir until bouillon dissolves and mixture comes to a boil. Reduce heat; simmer uncovered 15 minutes. Use to glaze chicken wings, frankfurters, meatballs, sliced beef or ham. Refrigerate leftovers.

MICROWAVE: In 1-quart glass measure, combine ingredients; mix well. Cook on 100% power (high) 4 to 6 minutes or until onion is tender, stirring every 2 minutes.

SALMON CANAPES

Makes 24 appetizers
36 calories per appetizer

1 (6½-ounce) can salmon, drained and flaked
1 tablespoon low-calorie mayonnaise
1 tablespoon ReaLemon® Lemon Juice from Concentrate
⅛ teaspoon dill weed
24 Melba rounds
6 slices Lite-line® Process Cheese Product,* any flavor, quartered
24 thin slices cucumber
Parsley

In small bowl, combine salmon, mayonnaise, ReaLemon and dill; mix well. On each Melba round, place a Lite-line piece, cucumber slice, 2 teaspoons salmon mixture and parsley. Serve immediately. Refrigerate leftovers.

*"½ the calories"—8% milk fat version.

Calories by product analyses and recipe calculation.

◄MARINATED VEGETABLES

Makes about 4 cups

4 cups assorted fresh vegetables
¼ cup ReaLemon® Lemon Juice from Concentrate
¼ cup vegetable oil
1 tablespoon sugar
1 teaspoon salt
½ teaspoon oregano or thyme leaves
⅛ teaspoon pepper

Place vegetables in 1½-quart shallow baking dish. In small bowl or jar, combine remaining ingredients; mix well. Pour over vegetables. Cover; refrigerate 6 hours or overnight, stirring occasionally. Serve as appetizer or on lettuce leaves as salad.

Suggested Vegetables: Cauliflowerets, carrots, mushrooms, cherry tomatoes, brussel sprouts, broccoli flowerets, zucchini, onion or cucumber.

Tip: Recipe can be doubled.

BEEF BARLEY VEGETABLE SOUP

Makes about 2½ quarts

1 pound beef shanks, cracked
7 cups water
1 (14½-ounce) can stewed tomatoes
¾ cup chopped onion
2 tablespoons Wyler's® Beef-Flavor Instant Bouillon or 6 Beef-Flavor Bouillon Cubes
½ teaspoon basil leaves
1 bay leaf
½ cup regular barley
1½ cups chopped carrots (3 medium)
1½ cups chopped celery

In large kettle or Dutch oven, combine shanks, water, tomatoes, onion, bouillon, basil and bay leaf. Bring to a boil. Reduce heat; cover and simmer 1 hour. Remove shanks from stock; cut meat into ½-inch pieces. Skim off fat. Add meat and barley; bring to a boil. Reduce heat; cover and simmer 30 minutes. Add carrots and celery; cook 30 minutes longer. Remove bay leaf. Refrigerate leftovers.

FROSTY STRAWBERRY LIME SOUP

Makes about 4 cups

1 pint fresh strawberries, cleaned and hulled
½ cup water
⅓ cup ReaLime® Lime Juice from Concentrate
⅓ cup sugar
1 (8-ounce) container Borden® Sour Cream or Plain Yogurt
Additional strawberries, optional

In blender container, combine strawberries, water, ReaLime and sugar; blend until smooth. In medium bowl, combine strawberry mixture and sour cream. Chill. Garnish with strawberries if desired. Refrigerate leftovers.

GOLDEN CAULIFLOWER SOUP

Makes 1½ to 2 quarts

2 (10-ounce) packages frozen cauliflower *or* 1 small head fresh cauliflower, separated into small flowerets (about 4 cups)
2 cups water
½ cup chopped onion
⅓ cup margarine or butter
⅓ to ½ cup unsifted flour
2 cups Borden® Milk
1 tablespoon Wyler's® Chicken-Flavor Instant Bouillon *or* 3 Chicken-Flavor Bouillon Cubes
2 cups (8 ounces) shredded mild Cheddar cheese
⅛ to ¼ teaspoon ground nutmeg
Chopped green onion or parsley

In medium saucepan, cook cauliflower in *1 cup* water until tender. Reserve *1 cup* cooked flowerets. In blender or food processor, blend remaining cauliflower and liquid; set aside. In large heavy saucepan, cook onion in margarine until tender; stir in flour. Gradually add remaining *1 cup* water, milk and bouillon; cook and stir until well blended and slightly thickened. Add cheese, pureed cauliflower, reserved flowerets and nutmeg; cook and stir until cheese melts and mixture is hot (do not boil). Garnish with green onion. Refrigerate leftovers.

ORIENTAL DIP

Makes about 2½ cups

1 cup mayonnaise or salad dressing
1 (8-ounce) container Borden® Sour Cream
1 (8-ounce) can water chestnuts, drained and finely chopped
2 tablespoons chopped pimiento
1 tablespoon sliced green onion
2 teaspoons Wyler's® Beef-Flavor Instant Bouillon
½ teaspoon Worcestershire sauce
¼ teaspoon garlic powder

In medium bowl, combine ingredients; mix well. Cover; chill to blend flavors. Stir before serving. Serve with Wise® Cottage Fries® Potato Chips. Refrigerate leftovers.

CHICKEN NOODLE SOUP

Makes about 3 quarts

4 cups diced cooked chicken *or* turkey
1 cup chopped celery
1 cup chopped onion
¼ cup margarine or butter
9 cups water
1 cup diced carrots
8 teaspoons Wyler's® Chicken-Flavor Instant Bouillon *or* 8 Chicken-Flavor Bouillon Cubes
½ teaspoon marjoram leaves
¼ to ½ teaspoon pepper
1 bay leaf
4 ounces uncooked Creamette® Medium Egg Noodles
1 tablespoon chopped parsley

In large kettle or Dutch oven, cook celery and onion in margarine until tender; add water, chicken, carrots, bouillon, marjoram, pepper and bay leaf. Bring to a boil. Reduce heat; cover and simmer 30 minutes. Remove bay leaf; add noodles and parsley. Cook 10 minutes longer or until noodles are tender. Refrigerate leftovers.

Top to Bottom: Chicken Noodle Soup, Golden Cauliflower Soup, Beef Barley Vegetable Soup

BEVERAGES

No matter the occasion, here's a bevy of beverages sure to offer one that's just right. These recipes range from spectacular party punches—spirited or not—refreshing wine coolers and fruit drinks to all-family shakes, creamy hot cocoa, warming winter sippers, holiday egg nog creations, even Homemade Irish Cream Liqueur.

ROSÉ WINE COOLER

Makes about 3½ quarts

Berry Mint Ice Ring, optional, or block of ice
1½ **cups sugar**
1 **cup ReaLemon® Lemon Juice from Concentrate**
2 **(750 mL) bottles rosé wine, chilled**
1 **(32-ounce) bottle club soda, chilled**

Prepare ice ring in advance. In large punch bowl, combine sugar and ReaLemon; stir until sugar dissolves. Just before serving, add wine, club soda and ice.

Berry Mint Ice Ring: Combine 3 cups water, 1 cup ReaLemon and ¾ cup sugar; stir until sugar dissolves. Pour 3 cups mixture into 6-cup ring mold; freeze. Arrange strawberries and mint leaves on top of ice. Slowly pour remaining ReaLemon mixture over fruit; freeze.

HOT TOMATO SIPPER

Makes about 1½ quarts

1 **tablespoon Wyler's® Beef-Flavor Instant Bouillon *or* 3 Beef-Flavor Bouillon Cubes**
1 **(46-ounce) can tomato juice**
2 **teaspoons prepared horseradish**
4 **drops hot pepper sauce**

Clockwise from Top: Rose Wine Cooler, Banana-Orange Shake, Bourbon Slush (see page 18), Hot Tomato Sipper, Melon Citrus Cooler (see page 18)

In large saucepan, combine ingredients; over low heat, simmer 10 minutes or until bouillon dissolves. Serve hot.

MICROWAVE: In 2-quart glass measure, combine ingredients. Heat on 100% power (high) 12 to 14 minutes or until hot and bouillon dissolves, stirring after 6 minutes.

BANANA SHAKE

Makes about 5 cups

2 **ripe bananas, cut up (about 2 cups)**
⅓ **cup ReaLemon® Lemon Juice from Concentrate**
1 **cup cold water**
1 **(14-ounce) can Eagle® Brand Sweetened Condensed Milk (NOT evaporated milk)**
2 **cups ice cubes**

In blender container, combine all ingredients except ice; blend well. Gradually add ice, blending until smooth. Garnish as desired. Refrigerate leftovers. (Mixture stays thick and creamy in refrigerator.)

Mixer Method: Omit ice cubes. In large mixer bowl, mash bananas; gradually beat in ReaLemon, sweetened condensed milk and 2½ cups cold water. Chill before serving.

Strawberry-Banana Shake: Reduce bananas to ½ cup; add 1½ cups fresh strawberries *or* 1 cup frozen unsweetened strawberries, partially thawed.

Banana-Orange Shake: Reduce bananas to 1 cup; use 1 cup orange juice instead of water.

Clockwise from Top: Chocolate Coconut Soda, Choco Cha Cha Shake, Creamy Hot Chocolate

CREAMY HOT CHOCOLATE

Makes about 2 quarts

1 (14-ounce) can Eagle® Brand Sweetened Condensed Milk (NOT evaporated milk)
½ cup unsweetened cocoa
1½ teaspoons vanilla extract
⅛ teaspoon salt
6½ cups hot water
Whipped cream, optional

In large saucepan, combine sweetened condensed milk, cocoa, vanilla and salt; mix well. Over medium heat, slowly stir in water; heat through, stirring occasionally. Garnish with whipped cream if desired.

CHOCOLATE COCONUT SODA

Makes 1 serving

¼ cup Coco Lopez® Cream of Coconut
2 tablespoons chocolate flavored syrup
2 scoops Borden® Chocolate or Vanilla Ice Cream
Club soda, chilled

In tall glass, mix together cream of coconut and syrup. Add ice cream and club soda. Stir. Garnish as desired. Serve immediately.

MELON CITRUS COOLER

Makes about 2 quarts

2 cups orange juice, chilled
½ cup ReaLemon® Lemon Juice from Concentrate
⅓ cup sugar
2 cups fresh or frozen melon balls
½ to 1 cup vodka, optional
2 (12-ounce) cans lemon-lime carbonated beverage, chilled
Ice

In pitcher, combine orange juice, ReaLemon and sugar; stir until sugar dissolves. Just before serving, add melon balls, vodka if desired and carbonated beverage. Serve over ice.

BOURBON SLUSH

Makes about 6 cups

2 cups brewed tea
1 (6-ounce) can frozen orange juice concentrate, thawed
⅓ cup sugar
2 cups cold water
1 cup bourbon
⅓ cup ReaLemon® Lemon Juice from Concentrate

In large bowl, combine tea, juice concentrate and sugar; stir until sugar dissolves. Add remaining ingredients. Freeze. About 1 hour before serving, remove from freezer; when mixture is slushy, spoon into cocktail glasses. Garnish as desired.

CHOCO CHA CHA SHAKE

Makes 1 serving

1 cup Borden® Milk
¼ cup Coco Lopez® Cream of Coconut
1 banana, sliced
1 tablespoon chocolate flavored syrup

In blender container, combine ingredients; blend until smooth. Garnish as desired.

Homemade Cream Liqueurs—Mint (left), Orange (center), Coffee (right)

HOMEMADE CREAM LIQUEURS

Makes about 1 quart

1 (14-ounce) can Eagle® Brand Sweetened Condensed Milk (NOT evaporated milk)
1¼ cups flavored liqueur (almond, coffee, orange *or* mint)
1 cup (½ pint) Borden® Whipping Cream or Coffee Cream
4 eggs*

In blender container, combine ingredients; blend until smooth. Store tightly covered in refrigerator up to 1 month. Stir before serving.

*Use only Grade A clean, uncracked eggs.

COFFEE EGG NOG PUNCH

Makes about 2½ quarts

2 (32-ounce) cans Borden® Egg Nog, chilled
¼ cup firmly packed light brown sugar
1 tablespoon instant coffee
¼ teaspoon ground cinnamon
½ cup coffee-flavored liqueur, optional
½ cup bourbon or brandy, optional
1 cup (½ pint) Borden® Whipping Cream
¼ cup confectioners' sugar
1 teaspoon vanilla extract
Cinnamon sticks and grated nutmeg, optional

In large bowl, combine egg nog, brown sugar, coffee and cinnamon; beat on low speed until sugar and coffee are dissolved. Stir in coffee liqueur and bourbon if desired; chill. In small bowl, beat cream with confectioners' sugar and vanilla until stiff. Pour egg nog into punch bowl; top with whipped cream and garnish with cinnamon sticks and nutmeg if desired. Refrigerate leftovers.

HOT COCOA MIX

Makes about 3 cups

1 cup Cremora™ Non-Dairy Creamer*
1 cup nonfat dry milk
¾ to 1 cup sugar
½ cup unsweetened cocoa

In medium bowl, combine ingredients; mix well. Store in airtight container. To serve, spoon 3 heaping tablespoons mix into mug; add ¾ cup boiling water. Stir.

Mocha: Add ¼ cup instant coffee.

Mexican: Add 1 teaspoon ground cinnamon.

Low Calorie: Omit sugar. Add 15 envelopes NutraSweet® low calorie sweetener *or* 2 teaspoons (5 envelopes) low-calorie granulated sugar substitute. To serve, spoon 2 heaping tablespoons mix into mug; add ¾ cup boiling water. Stir.

*Cremora is a coffee whitener and should not be used as a milk replacement.

◄RASPBERRY CHAMPAGNE PUNCH

Makes about 3 quarts

2 (10-ounce) packages frozen red
    raspberries in syrup, thawed
⅓ cup ReaLemon® Lemon Juice from
    Concentrate
½ cup sugar
1 (750 mL) bottle red rosé wine, chilled
1 quart Borden® Raspberry Sherbet
1 (750 mL) bottle dry champagne,
    chilled

In blender container, blend raspberries until
smooth. In large punch bowl, combine
raspberries, ReaLemon, sugar and wine; stir
until sugar dissolves. Just before serving,
scoop sherbet into punch bowl; add
champagne. Stir gently.

SOUTHERN SUNSHINE

Makes about 7 cups

2 cups orange juice
½ cup ReaLemon® Lemon Juice from
    Concentrate
¼ cup sugar
¾ cup Southern Comfort liqueur
1 (32-ounce) bottle lemon-lime
    carbonated beverage, chilled
  Ice

In pitcher, combine orange juice, ReaLemon
and sugar; stir until sugar dissolves. Just
before serving, add liqueur and carbonated
beverage; serve over ice. Garnish as desired.

HOMEMADE IRISH CREAM LIQUEUR

Makes about 5 cups

1¼ to 1¾ cups Irish whiskey, brandy,
    rum, bourbon, Scotch or rye
    whiskey
1 (14-ounce) can Eagle® Brand
    Sweetened Condensed Milk (NOT
    evaporated milk)
1 cup (½ pint) Borden® Whipping
    Cream or Coffee Cream
4 eggs*
2 tablespoons chocolate flavored syrup
2 teaspoons instant coffee
1 teaspoon vanilla extract
½ teaspoon almond extract

In blender container, combine ingredients;
blend until smooth. Store tightly covered in
refrigerator up to 1 month. Stir before serving.

*Use only Grade A clean, uncracked eggs.

WINE COOLER

Makes about 7 cups

3 cups dry white wine
½ cup ReaLemon® Lemon Juice from
    Concentrate
½ cup sugar
1 (32-ounce) bottle club soda, chilled
  Ice

In large pitcher, combine wine, ReaLemon and
sugar; stir until sugar dissolves. Just before
serving, add club soda. Serve over ice.

DOUBLE BERRY COCO PUNCH

Makes about 4 quarts

Ice Ring, optional, or block of ice
2 (10-ounce) packages frozen
    strawberries in syrup, thawed
1 (15-ounce) can Coco Lopez® Cream of
    Coconut
1 (48-ounce) bottle cranberry juice
    cocktail, chilled
2 cups light rum, optional
1 (32-ounce) bottle club soda, chilled
    Fresh strawberries and mint leaves,
    optional

Prepare ice ring in advance. In blender container, blend thawed strawberries and cream of coconut until smooth. In large punch bowl, combine strawberry mixture, cranberry juice and rum if desired. Just before serving, add club soda and ice. Garnish with fresh strawberries and mint if desired.

Ice Ring: Fill ring mold with water to within 1 inch of top rim; freeze. Arrange strawberries, cranberries, mint leaves, lime slices or other fruits on top of ice. Carefully pour small amount of cold water over fruits; freeze.

Ambrosia Punch (top), Double Berry Coco Punch (bottom)

PINA COLADA PUNCH

Makes about 4 quarts

Ice Ring, optional, or block of ice
1 (20-ounce) can crushed pineapple,
    undrained
2 (15-ounce) cans Coco Lopez® Cream of
    Coconut
1 (46-ounce) can pineapple juice,
    chilled
2 cups light rum, optional
1 (32-ounce) bottle club soda, chilled

Prepare ice ring in advance. In blender container, blend crushed pineapple and cream of coconut until smooth. In large punch bowl, combine pineapple mixture, pineapple juice and rum if desired. Just before serving, add club soda and ice.

Ice Ring: Fill ring mold with water to within 1 inch of top rim; freeze. Arrange pineapple chunks and maraschino cherries on top of ice. Carefully pour small amount of cold water over fruits; freeze.

AMBROSIA PUNCH

Makes about 3 quarts

Ice Ring, optional, or block of ice
2 cups apricot nectar, chilled
2 cups orange juice, chilled
2 cups pineapple juice, chilled
1 (15-ounce) can Coco Lopez® Cream of
    Coconut
1½ cups light rum, optional
1 (32-ounce) bottle club soda, chilled

Prepare ice ring in advance. In punch bowl, combine all ingredients except club soda and ice ring; mix well. Just before serving, add club soda and ice.

Ice Ring: Fill ring mold with water to within 1 inch of top rim; freeze. Arrange grapes, apricot halves, mint leaves, maraschino cherries or other fruits on top of ice. Carefully pour small amount of cold water over fruits; freeze.

◄SPIRITED COFFEE LOPEZ

Makes 5 cups

4 cups hot coffee
½ cup Coco Lopez® Cream of Coconut
½ cup Irish whiskey
1 teaspoon vanilla extract
Whipped cream

In heat-proof pitcher, combine all ingredients except whipped cream; mix well. Pour into mugs; top with whipped cream. Serve immediately.

SIMMERED SHERRY BOUILLON

Makes about 2 quarts

8 cups water
3 tablespoons Wyler's® Beef-Flavor Instant Bouillon *or* 9 Beef-Flavor Bouillon Cubes
⅓ cup dry sherry
Lemon slices, optional

In large saucepan, bring water and bouillon to a boil; stir until bouillon dissolves. Remove from heat; stir in sherry. Serve hot. Garnish with lemon slices if desired.

MICROWAVE: In 2-quart glass measure, heat water and bouillon on 100% power (high) 10 to 14 minutes or until boiling. Stir until bouillon dissolves. Proceed as above.

FRUIT MEDLEY PUNCH

Makes about 3½ quarts

Ice block or ice ring
2 (10-ounce) packages frozen strawberries in syrup, thawed
3 cups apricot nectar, chilled
3 cups cold water
1 cup ReaLemon® Lemon Juice from Concentrate
1 (6-ounce) can frozen orange juice concentrate, thawed
1 cup sugar
3 (12-ounce) cans ginger ale, chilled

Prepare ice block in advance. In blender container, puree strawberries. In large punch bowl, combine pureed strawberries and remaining ingredients except ginger ale and ice ring; stir until sugar dissolves. Just before serving, add ginger ale and ice.

PINEAPPLE TEA

Makes about 2 quarts

2 tablespoons unsweetened instant tea
½ cup sugar
1 cup hot water
4 cups pineapple juice, chilled
1½ cups cold water
½ cup ReaLemon® Lemon Juice from Concentrate
Ice

In pitcher, combine tea, sugar and hot water; stir until sugar dissolves. Add pineapple juice, cold water and ReaLemon; serve over ice. Garnish as desired.

PEACH DAIQUIRIS

Makes about 1 quart

  3 cups pared sliced fresh peaches
  ½ cup light rum
  ¼ cup ReaLime® Lime Juice from
     Concentrate
  ⅓ cup granulated sugar
  2 cups ice cubes

In blender container, combine all ingredients except ice; blend well. Gradually add ice, blending until smooth. Garnish as desired.

Tip: 1 (16-ounce) package frozen unsweetened peaches, partially thawed, can be substituted for fresh peaches; increase sugar to ½ cup.

BANANA DAIQUIRIS

Makes about 2½ cups

  2 ripe medium bananas, sliced
  ⅓ cup confectioners' sugar
  ⅓ cup light rum
  3 tablespoons ReaLime® Lime Juice
     from Concentrate
  2 cups ice cubes

In blender container, combine all ingredients except ice; blend well. Gradually add ice, blending until smooth.

RAINBOW PARTY PUNCH

Makes about 3½ quarts

  1 (4-serving size) package lemon, lime,
     orange, raspberry or strawberry
     flavor gelatin
1½ cups sugar
  2 cups boiling water
  1 (46-ounce) can pineapple juice,
     chilled
  2 cups ReaLemon® Lemon Juice from
     Concentrate
  1 quart Borden® Sherbet, any flavor
  1 (32-ounce) bottle club soda, chilled

In medium bowl, dissolve gelatin and sugar in boiling water; set aside. In large bowl, combine pineapple juice, ReaLemon and gelatin mixture. Chill. Just before serving, pour juice mixture into punch bowl; add sherbet and club soda.

Peach Daiquiri (left), Banana Daiquiri (right)

LEMONADE

Makes 1 quart

  ½ cup sugar
  ½ cup ReaLemon® Lemon Juice from
     Concentrate
3¼ cups cold water

In large pitcher, dissolve sugar in ReaLemon; add water. Serve over ice. Garnish as desired.

Sparkling Lemonade: Substitute club soda for cold water.

Slushy Lemonade: In blender container, combine ReaLemon and sugar with ½ cup water. Gradually add 4 cups ice cubes, blending until smooth. Serve immediately.

Pink Lemonade: Stir in 1 to 2 teaspoons grenadine syrup *or* 1 to 2 drops red food coloring.

Minted Lemonade: Stir in 2 to 3 drops peppermint extract.

Low Calorie: Omit sugar. Add 4 to 8 envelopes sugar substitute or 1½ teaspoons liquid sugar substitute.

SALADS & SIDE DISHES

Brighten up a buffet with a colorful fruit or vegetable salad, or take a tossed salad out-of-the-ordinary with a quick homemade dressing. Make a hearty main dish salad the star of the meal. Or round out the menu with a savory pasta, rice or vegetable side dish.

◄CELERY SEED DRESSING

Makes about 1 cup

½ cup sugar
¼ cup ReaLemon® Lemon Juice from Concentrate
2 teaspoons cider vinegar
1 teaspoon dry mustard
½ teaspoon salt
½ cup vegetable oil
1 teaspoon celery seed or poppy seed

In blender container, combine all ingredients except oil and celery seed; blend until smooth. On low speed, continue blending, slowly adding oil. Stir in celery seed. Chill to blend flavors. Refrigerate leftovers.

BROCCOLI WITH CHOWDER SAUCE

Makes 8 servings

2 (10-ounce) packages frozen broccoli spears, cooked and well drained
1 (15-ounce) can Snow's® or Doxsee Condensed New England Clam Chowder
¼ cup Borden® Sour Cream or Milk
½ cup (2 ounces) shredded Cheddar cheese

Preheat oven to 325°. Arrange broccoli in lightly greased 8-inch square baking dish. In small bowl, combine chowder and sour cream; spoon over broccoli. Bake 20 minutes. Remove from oven; sprinkle with cheese. Return to oven 5 minutes or until cheese melts. Refrigerate leftovers.

MICROWAVE: In 2-quart round baking dish, combine frozen broccoli and ¼ cup water; cover. Cook on 100% power (high) 7 to 9 minutes. Drain. Arrange broccoli in lightly greased 8-inch square baking dish. Combine chowder and sour cream; spoon over broccoli. Cover; cook on 100% power (high) 5 to 7 minutes or until hot. Top with cheese during last 2 minutes.

SEASONED RICE

Makes 6 servings

1 tablespoon Wyler's® Beef- or Chicken-Flavor Instant Bouillon *or* 3 Beef- or Chicken-Flavor Bouillon Cubes
2 to 2½ cups water
1 cup uncooked long grain rice
1 tablespoon margarine or vegetable oil
1 tablespoon chopped parsley

In medium saucepan, combine bouillon and water; bring to a boil. Add remaining ingredients; return to a boil. Reduce heat; cover and simmer 15 to 20 minutes or until rice is tender and liquid is absorbed.

MARINATED ORIENTAL BEEF SALAD

Makes 4 servings

1 (1- to 1¼-pound) flank steak
⅓ cup ReaLemon® Lemon Juice from
   Concentrate
¼ cup catsup
¼ cup vegetable oil
1 tablespoon brown sugar
¼ teaspoon garlic powder
¼ teaspoon ground ginger
¼ teaspoon pepper
8 ounces fresh mushrooms, sliced
   (about 2 cups)
1 (8-ounce) can sliced water chestnuts,
   drained
1 medium sweet onion, sliced and
   separated into rings
1 (6-ounce) package frozen pea pods,
   thawed, or 4 ounces fresh pea pods
   Lettuce leaves
   Tomato wedges

Broil meat 5 minutes on each side or until desired doneness; slice diagonally into thin strips. Meanwhile, in large bowl, combine ReaLemon, catsup, oil, sugar, garlic powder, ginger and pepper; mix well. Add sliced meat, mushrooms, water chestnuts and onion; mix well. Cover; refrigerate 8 hours or overnight, stirring occasionally. Before serving, add pea pods. Serve on lettuce; garnish with tomato. Refrigerate leftovers.

AMBROSIA FRUIT DIP

Makes about 1⅓ cups

1 (8-ounce) container Borden®
   Lite-line® Fruit Yogurt, any
   flavor
½ cup Coco Lopez® Cream of Coconut
¼ cup chopped pecans, toasted

In small bowl, combine yogurt and cream of coconut; mix well. Stir in nuts; chill. Serve with fresh fruit. Refrigerate leftovers.

Tip: For Ambrosia Fruit Salad, toss sauce with 8 to 10 cups cut-up assorted fresh fruit.

Marinated Oriental Beef Salad

GOLDEN SQUASH BAKE ▶

Makes 6 to 8 servings

**8 cups sliced yellow summer squash,
cooked and drained**
6 slices bacon, cooked and crumbled
2 eggs
1 cup Borden® Cottage Cheese
2 tablespoons flour
**2 teaspoons Wyler's® Chicken-Flavor
Instant Bouillon**
**1 cup (4 ounces) shredded sharp
Cheddar cheese**

Preheat oven to 350°. In large bowl, combine
eggs, cottage cheese, flour and bouillon. Add
squash; mix well. Turn into greased 12×7-inch
baking dish. Top with Cheddar cheese and
bacon. Bake 20 to 25 minutes. Let stand 5
minutes before serving. Refrigerate leftovers.

CREAMY GREEN BEANS ALMONDINE

Makes 6 servings

**2 (9-ounce) packages frozen green
beans, cooked and drained**
2 tablespoons margarine or butter
2 tablespoons flour
**2 teaspoons Wyler's® Chicken-Flavor
Instant Bouillon _or_ 2 Chicken-
Flavor Bouillon Cubes**
¾ cup Borden® Milk
**½ cup (2 ounces) shredded Mozzarella
cheese**
¼ cup sliced almonds, toasted if desired

In medium saucepan, melt margarine; stir in
flour and bouillon. Gradually stir in milk; cook
and stir until thickened. Add cheese; stir until
melted. Add beans; heat through. Stir in
almonds. Serve immediately. Refrigerate
leftovers.

MICROWAVE: In 2-cup glass measure, melt
margarine on 100% power (high) 30 seconds.
Stir in flour and bouillon. Gradually stir in
milk. Cook on 100% power (high) 3 to 3½
minutes, stirring after each minute, until
thick and bubbly. Add cheese; stir until cheese
melts. Add beans; cook on 100% power (high)
1 to 2 minutes or until heated through. Stir in
almonds.

POTATOES AND ZUCCHINI AU GRATIN

Makes 6 to 8 servings

**1 pound potatoes, cooked, peeled and
sliced (about 3 cups)**
**3 cups sliced zucchini, cooked (about 1
pound)**
3 tablespoons margarine or butter
3 tablespoons flour
**1 tablespoon Wyler's® Chicken-Flavor
Instant Bouillon _or_ 3 Chicken-
Flavor Bouillon Cubes**
1½ cups Borden® Milk
**1 cup (4 ounces) shredded mild
Cheddar cheese**
2 tablespoons chopped pimiento
**½ teaspoon thyme leaves
Canned French fried onions**

Preheat oven to 350°. In medium saucepan,
over medium heat, melt margarine; stir in
flour and bouillon. Gradually stir in milk. Cook
and stir until thickened and bouillon is
dissolved. Remove from heat; add cheese,
pimiento and thyme; stir until cheese melts. In
1½-quart baking dish, layer half each of the
potatoes, zucchini and sauce; repeat layering.
Bake 25 minutes or until bubbly. Top with
onions; bake 2 minutes longer. Refrigerate
leftovers.

CREAMY FETTUCCINI TOSS

Makes 6 to 8 servings

¼ cup margarine or butter
1 tablespoon flour
2 teaspoons Wyler's Chicken-Flavor
    Instant Bouillon
¾ teaspoon basil leaves
¼ teaspoon garlic powder
⅛ teaspoon pepper
1 cup (½ pint) Borden® Coffee Cream
    or Half-and-Half
1 cup Borden® Milk
½ (1-pound) package Creamette®
    Fettuccini
¼ cup grated Parmesan cheese
    Chopped parsley, walnuts and
    cooked crumbled bacon

In medium saucepan, over medium heat, melt margarine; stir in flour, bouillon, basil, garlic powder and pepper. Gradually add cream and milk. Cook and stir until bouillon dissolves and sauce thickens slightly, about 15 minutes. Meanwhile, cook fettuccini as package directs; drain. Remove sauce from heat; add cheese. In large bowl, pour sauce over *hot* fettuccini; stir to coat. Garnish with parsley, walnuts and bacon. Serve immediately. Refrigerate leftovers.

LEMON VINAIGRETTE DRESSING

Makes about 1 cup

½ cup vegetable oil
⅓ cup ReaLemon® Lemon Juice from
    Concentrate
¼ cup sliced green onions
1 tablespoon Dijon-style mustard
1 teaspoon sugar
½ teaspoon salt

In 1-pint jar with tight-fitting lid or cruet, combine all ingredients; shake well. Chill to blend flavors. Use as a salad dressing or as a marinade for asparagus, broccoli, poultry or fish.

CITRUS CHEESE SALAD

Makes 1 serving
200 calories

½ cup Borden® Lite-line® Cottage
    Cheese
1 slice Lite-line® Process Cheese
    Product,* any flavor, cut into small
    pieces
2 tablespoons chopped cucumber
½ fresh grapefruit, pared and sectioned
    Lettuce leaf

In small bowl, combine cottage cheese, Lite-line pieces and cucumber. On salad plate, arrange grapefruit on lettuce. Top with cheese mixture. Refrigerate leftovers.

*"½ the calories"—8% milk fat product.

Calories by product analyses and recipe calculation.

MEXICAN TOSSED SALAD

Makes 8 servings

3 large ripe avocados, seeded, peeled
    and sliced
½ cup Borden® Sour Cream
¼ cup ReaLemon® Lemon Juice from
    Concentrate
1 tablespoon finely chopped onion
1 tablespoon water
¼ teaspoon salt
¼ teaspoon hot pepper sauce
6 cups torn mixed salad greens
1 large tomato, seeded and chopped
1 cup (4 ounces) shredded mild
    Cheddar or Monterey Jack cheese
½ cup sliced pitted black olives
1 cup coarsely crushed tortilla chips

In medium bowl, mash *1 avocado;* stir in sour cream, *3 tablespoons* ReaLemon, onion, water, salt and hot pepper sauce. Chill to blend flavors. In large bowl, sprinkle remaining *2 avocados* with remaining *1 tablespoon* ReaLemon. Top with salad greens, tomato, cheese and olives; chill. Just before serving, toss with avocado dressing and tortilla chips.

CALIFORNIA CAESAR SALAD

Makes 6 servings

½ cup vegetable oil
⅓ cup ReaLemon® Lemon Juice from Concentrate
1 egg,* beaten
2 cloves garlic, finely chopped
2 medium heads romaine lettuce, torn into bite-size pieces (about 8 cups)
2 medium tomatoes, seeded and diced
1 ripe avocado, seeded, peeled and sliced
⅓ cup grated Parmesan cheese
¼ cup sliced green onions
1 cup garlic croutons
¼ cup imitation bacon or cooked crumbled bacon

In 1-pint jar with tight-fitting lid or cruet, combine oil, ReaLemon, egg and garlic; shake well. Chill to blend flavors. Just before serving, in large bowl, combine remaining ingredients. Toss with dressing. Refrigerate leftovers.

*Use only Grade A clean, uncracked egg.

SAVORY STUFFED SQUASH

Makes 4 servings

2 medium acorn squash, halved and seeded
1 cup finely chopped celery
½ cup chopped onion
2 tablespoons margarine or butter
1⅓ cups (one-half 28-ounce jar) None Such® Ready-to-Use Mincemeat (Regular *or* Brandy & Rum)
Melted margarine or butter
Salt and pepper, optional

Preheat oven to 350°. Place squash, cut-side down, in large shallow baking dish. Bake 35 minutes. Meanwhile, in small skillet, cook celery and onion in *2 tablespoons* margarine until tender. Stir in mincemeat; heat through. Remove squash from oven; turn cut-side up. Fill squash halves with mincemeat mixture; brush cut edges with melted margarine. Bake an additional 20 to 25 minutes or until tender. Brush with additional melted margarine to prevent drying during baking. Season with salt and pepper if desired. Refrigerate leftovers.

California Caesar Salad

TACO SALAD ▲

Makes 4 servings

- 1 pound lean ground beef
- 1 (14½-ounce) can stewed tomatoes
- 1 (4-ounce) can chopped mild green chilies, drained
- 2 teaspoons Wyler's® Beef-Flavor Instant Bouillon *or* 2 Beef-Flavor Bouillon Cubes
- ¼ teaspoon hot pepper sauce
- ⅛ teaspoon garlic powder Dash pepper
- 1 medium head lettuce, shredded (1 quart)
- 1 to 1½ cups corn chips
- 1 cup (4 ounces) shredded Cheddar cheese
- 1 medium tomato, chopped (about 1 cup)

In large skillet, brown meat; pour off fat. Add stewed tomatoes, chilies, bouillon, hot pepper sauce, garlic powder and pepper; simmer uncovered 30 minutes. In large bowl or platter, arrange lettuce then meat mixture, chips, cheese and tomato. Refrigerate leftovers.

SAVORY LEMON VEGETABLES

Makes 8 servings

- 6 slices bacon, cooked and crumbled, reserving ¼ cup drippings
- 1 pound carrots, pared and sliced
- 1 medium head cauliflower, core removed
- 1 cup finely chopped onion
- ½ cup ReaLemon® Lemon Juice from Concentrate
- ½ cup water
- 4 teaspoons sugar
- 1 teaspoon salt
- 1 teaspoon thyme leaves Chopped parsley

In large saucepan, cook carrots and cauliflower in small amount of water until tender. Meanwhile, in medium skillet, cook onion in reserved drippings. Add ReaLemon, *½ cup water*, sugar, salt and thyme; bring to a boil. Drain vegetables; arrange on serving dish. Pour warm sauce over vegetables. Garnish with bacon and parsley. Refrigerate leftovers.

READY GRAVY MIX

Makes about 2 cups mix

GRAVY MIX:
1 (2¼-ounce) jar Wyler's® Beef- *or*
    Chicken-Flavor Instant Bouillon
    (about ½ cup)
1½ cups unsifted flour
½ teaspoon pepper

In medium bowl, stir together all ingredients.
Store in 1-pint jar with tight-fitting lid at room
temperature. Shake or stir before using.

GRAVY:
¼ cup Ready Gravy Mix
3 tablespoons margarine, melted, *or*
    drippings
1¾ cups water or milk

In medium skillet or saucepan, stir gravy mix
into margarine; cook and stir until golden
brown. Add water; cook and stir until
thickened and bouillon dissolves. (Makes about
1¾ cups)

PARTY CHICKEN MACARONI SALAD

Makes 8 to 10 servings

3 cups cubed cooked chicken or turkey
1 (7-ounce) package *or* 2 cups uncooked
    Creamettes® Elbow Macaroni,
    cooked as package directs, rinsed
    and drained
1 cup chopped celery
1 tablespoon grated orange rind
2 medium oranges, peeled and
    sectioned
1 cup seedless green grape halves
½ to 1 cup mayonnaise or salad dressing
½ to 1 cup Borden® Sour Cream
1 tablespoon Wyler's® Chicken-Flavor
    Instant Bouillon
3 tablespoons sliced maraschino
    cherries
    Lettuce leaves
½ cup toasted nuts

In large bowl, combine all ingredients except
cherries, lettuce and nuts. Mix well. Chill
thoroughly. Just before serving, stir in
cherries. Serve on lettuce; garnish with nuts.
Refrigerate leftovers.

FRUITED AMBROSIA

Makes 10 to 12 servings

1 (14-ounce) can Eagle® Brand
    Sweetened Condensed Milk (NOT
    evaporated milk)
1 (8-ounce) container Borden®
    Lite-line® Plain Yogurt
½ cup ReaLime® Lime Juice from
    Concentrate
2 (11-ounce) cans mandarin orange
    segments, drained
1 (20-ounce) can pineapple chunks,
    drained
1½ cups grape halves (about ½ pound)
1 (3½-ounce) can flaked coconut
    (1⅓ cups)
1 cup Campfire® Miniature
    Marshmallows
1 cup chopped pecans or walnuts,
    optional
½ cup sliced maraschino cherries, well
    drained

In large bowl, combined sweetened condensed
milk, yogurt and ReaLime; mix well. Stir in
remaining ingredients. Chill 3 hours or longer
to blend flavors. Garnish as desired.
Refrigerate leftovers.

Fruited Ambrosia

MAIN DISHES

Chicken and turkey, beef, fish, pork and ham—all are included in this medley of main dishes. Feature all-American ground beef in a traditional meat loaf, Meatza Pizzas or Cheeseburger Pie. Vary the menu with a variety of versatile chicken creations, savory sandwiches, zesty chili or hearty stews.

◀ VERSATILE CHICKEN

Makes 4 to 6 servings

1 (2½- to 3-pound) broiler-fryer
    chicken, cut up
¾ cup Borden® Buttermilk
1 tablespoon Wyler's® Chicken-Flavor
    Instant Bouillon
½ teaspoon oregano leaves, optional
1 cup unsifted flour
1 teaspoon paprika
¼ cup margarine or butter, melted

In 1-cup measure, combine buttermilk, bouillon and oregano if desired; mix well. Let stand 10 minutes; stir. Place chicken in large bowl. Pour bouillon mixture over chicken; toss to coat. Let stand 30 minutes to blend flavors. In paper or plastic bag, combine flour and paprika. Add chicken, a few pieces at a time; shake to coat. Place in 13×9-inch baking dish. Drizzle with margarine. Bake uncovered in preheated 350° oven 1 hour or until golden. Refrigerate leftovers.

Tip: To fry chicken, omit melted margarine; fry in vegetable oil.

TANGY COCONUT HAM GLAZE

Makes about ¾ cup,
enough to glaze a 10- to 12-pound ham

¾ cup Coco Lopez® Cream of Coconut
2 tablespoons prepared mustard
1½ teaspoons cornstarch

In small saucepan, combine ingredients; bring to a boil. Cook and stir 2 to 3 minutes or until thickened. Use to glaze ham during last 30 minutes of baking.

MICROWAVE: In 2-cup glass measure, combine ingredients. Cook on 70% power (medium-high) 4 to 6 minutes or until thickened, stirring every 2 minutes. Let stand 5 minutes. Proceed as above.

ALL-AMERICAN MEAT LOAF

Makes 8 servings

8 slices Borden® Process American
    Cheese Food
2 pounds lean ground beef
1¼ cups dry bread crumbs
¾ cup catsup
2 eggs
1 (1.5-ounce) package Mrs. Grass®
    Onion Dip 'n Soup 'n Recipe Mix

Preheat oven to 350° (325° for glass dish). Cut *6 slices* cheese food into small pieces; combine with remaining ingredients. Mix well. In shallow baking pan, shape into loaf. Bake 1 hour. Remove from oven; arrange remaining cheese food slices on top. Return to oven 5 minutes or until cheese food begins to melt. Refrigerate leftovers.

CHUCKWAGON ROAST AND VEGETABLES

Makes 6 to 8 servings

1 (3-pound) boneless beef chuck roast
2 tablespoons vegetable oil
3 tablespoons flour
1 cup Borden® Buttermilk
1 cup water
4 teaspoons Wyler's® Beef-Flavor
    Instant Bouillon *or* 4 Beef-Flavor
    Bouillon Cubes
½ teaspoon thyme leaves
¼ teaspoon pepper
4 medium carrots, cut into 1-inch
    pieces
2 medium onions, cut into wedges
1 (10-ounce) package frozen broccoli
    spears, thawed and cut into pieces
1 (10-ounce) package frozen
    cauliflower, thawed

Preheat oven to 350°. In large skillet, brown roast in oil. Place in 3-quart roasting or baking pan. Add flour to drippings in skillet; cook and stir until browned. Add buttermilk, water, bouillon, thyme and pepper. Cook and stir until bouillon dissolves and mixture thickens slightly, about 10 minutes. Place carrots and onions around meat; spoon sauce over meat. Cover; bake 1 hour and 45 minutes or until meat is tender. Add remaining vegetables; bake 10 minutes longer or until tender. Refrigerate leftovers.

CRANBERRY GLAZED PORK ROAST

Makes 10 to 12 servings

1 (3½- to 4-pound) boneless pork loin
    roast
  Salt and pepper
1 (16-ounce) can whole berry cranberry
    sauce
¼ cup ReaLemon® Lemon Juice from
    Concentrate
3 tablespoons brown sugar
1 teaspoon cornstarch

Preheat oven to 450°. Place meat in shallow baking dish; season with salt and pepper. Roast 20 minutes. Reduce oven temperature to 325°; continue roasting. Meanwhile, in small saucepan, combine remaining ingredients. Over medium heat, cook and stir until slightly thickened, about 5 minutes. After meat has cooked 1 hour, drain off fat; spoon half of the sauce over meat. Continue roasting 1 to 1½ hours or until meat thermometer reaches 160°, basting occasionally. Spoon remaining sauce over meat; return to oven 10 to 15 minutes. Let stand 10 minutes before slicing. Refrigerate leftovers.

To Make Gravy: In small saucepan, combine meat drippings and 2 tablespoons cornstarch. Over medium heat, cook and stir until thickened, about 5 minutes. (Makes about 2 cups)

Chuckwagon Roast and Vegetables

CHICKEN ENCHILADAS

Makes 6 to 8 servings

  3 cups finely chopped cooked chicken
  1 cup chopped onion
  ¼ cup margarine or butter
  ¼ cup unsifted flour
  2½ cups hot water
  1 tablespoon Wyler's® Chicken-Flavor
       Instant Bouillon *or* 3 Chicken-
       Flavor Bouillon Cubes
  1 (8-ounce) container Borden® Sour
       Cream, at room temperature
  2 cups (8 ounces) shredded Cheddar
       cheese
  1 (4-ounce) can chopped mild green
       chilies, drained
  1 teaspoon ground cumin
 12 (6-inch) corn tortillas *or* 10 (8-inch)
       flour tortillas
     Sour cream, chopped green onions
       and chopped tomato for garnish

Preheat oven to 350°. In medium saucepan,
cook onion in margarine until tender. Stir in
flour then water and bouillon; cook and stir
until thickened and bouillon dissolves. Remove
from heat; stir in sour cream. In large bowl,
combine *1 cup* sauce, chicken, *1 cup* cheese,
chilies and cumin; mix well. Dip each tortilla
into remaining hot sauce to soften; fill each
with equal portions of chicken mixture. Roll
up. Arrange in greased 13×9-inch baking dish.
Spoon remaining sauce over. Sprinkle with
remaining cheese. Bake 25 minutes or until
bubbly. Garnish as desired. Refrigerate
leftovers.

MICROWAVE: In 2-quart round baking dish,
melt margarine on 100% power (high) 1
minute. Add onion; cook on 100% power (high)
3 to 5 minutes or until tender. Stir in flour,
then water and bouillon; cook on 100% power
(high) 8 minutes, or until thickened and
bouillon dissolves, stirring every 2 minutes.
Stir in sour cream. Proceed as above. Arrange
rolled tortillas in greased 12×7-inch baking
dish. Cook on 70% power (medium-high) 9
minutes or until bubbly. Let stand 5 minutes
before serving.

SALMON CHEESE PUFF PIES ▲

Makes 6 servings

  1 (15½-ounce) can salmon, drained and
       flaked
  1 cup Borden® Cottage Cheese
  ¼ cup chopped green pepper
  ¼ cup chopped onion
  3 tablespoons ReaLemon® Lemon Juice
       from Concentrate
  1 (2-ounce) jar pimientos, drained and
       chopped
  ¼ teaspoon dill weed
  1 (10-ounce) package frozen puff pastry
       patty shells, thawed in refrigerator
       overnight

Preheat oven to 450°. In large bowl, combine
all ingredients except patty shells. On floured
surface, roll each shell to an 8-inch circle. Place
equal amounts of salmon mixture in center of
each circle. Fold over; seal edges with water
and press with fork. Place on ungreased
baking sheet; cut slit near center of each
turnover. Reduce oven temperature to 400°;
bake 25 minutes or until golden brown.
Refrigerate leftovers.

DEEP DISH TURKEY PIE

Makes 6 servings

3 cups cubed cooked turkey *or* chicken
1 cup sliced cooked carrots
1 cup cubed cooked potatoes
1 cup frozen green peas, thawed
6 tablespoons margarine or butter
⅓ cup unsifted flour
2 tablespoons Wyler's® Chicken-Flavor Instant Bouillon *or* 6 Chicken-Flavor Bouillon Cubes
¼ teaspoon pepper
4 cups Borden® Milk
2¼ cups biscuit baking mix

Preheat oven to 375°. In large saucepan, melt margarine; stir in flour, bouillon and pepper. Over medium heat, gradually add milk; cook and stir until mixture thickens. Add remaining ingredients except biscuit mix; mix well. Pour into 2½-quart baking dish. Prepare biscuit mix according to package directions for rolled biscuits. Roll out to cover dish; cut slashes in center of dough. Place on top of dish; crimp edges. Bake 40 minutes or until golden. Refrigerate leftovers.

HOMEMADE PORK AND POULTRY COATING MIX

Makes about 1½ cups

1½ cups plain dry bread crumbs
4 teaspoons Wyler's® Chicken-Flavor Instant Bouillon
1 teaspoon paprika
1 teaspoon poultry seasoning
¾ teaspoon oregano leaves
½ teaspoon garlic powder
¼ to ½ teaspoon pepper

In medium bowl, combine all ingredients; mix well. Store in airtight container at room temperature.

To Use: Dip chicken or chops in melted margarine or milk; coat with mix; bake in preheated 375° oven until tender (about 1 hour for chicken *or* 35 to 40 minutes for chops). Refrigerate leftovers.

SWISS CHICKEN QUICHE ▲

Makes 6 servings

2 cups cubed cooked chicken *or* turkey
1 (9-inch) unbaked pastry shell, pricked
1 cup (4 ounces) shredded Swiss cheese
2 tablespoons flour
1 tablespoon Wyler's® Chicken-Flavor Instant Bouillon
1 cup Borden® Milk
3 eggs, well beaten
¼ cup chopped onion
2 tablespoons chopped green pepper
2 tablespoons chopped pimiento

Preheat oven to 425°. Bake pastry shell 8 minutes; remove from oven. Reduce oven temperature to 350°. In medium bowl, toss cheese with flour and bouillon; add remaining ingredients. Mix well. Pour into prepared shell. Bake 40 to 45 minutes or until set. Let stand 10 minutes before serving. Garnish as desired. Refrigerate leftovers.

SHRIMP AND SAUSAGE JAMBALAYA ▲

Makes 8 servings

1 pound medium raw shrimp, peeled, leaving tails on and deveined
1 pound smoked or Italian sausage, cut into ½-inch slices
1 cup cubed cooked ham
1 cup chopped onion
¾ cup chopped green pepper
1 clove garlic, finely chopped
3 tablespoons vegetable oil
3¼ cups water
1 (28-ounce) can whole tomatoes, undrained and broken up
2 cups uncooked long grain rice
4 teaspoons Wyler's® Chicken- or Beef-Flavor Instant Bouillon or 4 Chicken- or Beef-Flavor Bouillon Cubes
2 to 3 teaspoons paprika
¼ teaspoon basil leaves
¼ teaspoon thyme leaves
⅛ teaspoon pepper
 Chopped parsley
 Hot pepper sauce, optional

In large kettle or Dutch oven, cook sausage, ham, onion, green pepper and garlic in oil until sausage browns. Stir in remaining ingredients except shrimp, parsley and hot pepper sauce; bring to a boil. Reduce heat; cover and simmer 20 minutes. Stir in shrimp; cook uncovered 5 to 8 minutes longer or until liquid is almost absorbed. Garnish with parsley. Serve with hot pepper sauce if desired. Refrigerate leftovers.

LIVELY LEMON ROLL-UPS

Makes 8 servings

1 cup cooked rice
⅓ cup margarine or butter
⅓ cup ReaLemon® Lemon Juice from Concentrate
2 teaspoons salt
¼ teaspoon pepper
1 (10-ounce) package frozen chopped broccoli, thawed and well drained
1 cup (4 ounces) shredded Cheddar cheese
8 fish fillets, fresh or frozen, thawed (about 2 pounds)
 Paprika

Preheat oven to 375°. In small saucepan, melt margarine; add ReaLemon, salt and pepper. In medium bowl, combine rice, broccoli, cheese and ¼ cup ReaLemon sauce; mix well. Divide broccoli mixture equally among fillets. Roll up and place seam-side down in shallow 2-quart baking dish. Pour remaining ReaLemon sauce over roll-ups. Bake 25 minutes or until fish flakes with fork. Spoon sauce over individual servings; garnish with paprika. Refrigerate leftovers.

MICROWAVE: Prepare fish as above. Arrange in 12 × 7-inch baking dish; cover with plastic wrap. Cook on 100% power (high) 10 to 12 minutes or until fish flakes with fork, rotating dish once. Serve as above.

Lively Lemon Roll-Ups

MEATZA PIZZAS

Makes 8 to 10 servings

2 pounds lean ground beef
½ cup finely chopped onion
½ cup fresh bread crumbs (1 slice bread)
2 eggs
4 teaspoons Wyler's® Beef-Flavor Instant Bouillon
¼ teaspoon garlic powder
1 (6-ounce) can tomato paste
½ teaspoon oregano leaves
½ teaspoon sugar
Toppings:
    Sliced mushrooms
    Chopped green pepper
    Sliced pepperoni
    Cooked crumbled bacon
Shredded Mozzarella cheese

In large bowl, combine meat, onion, crumbs, eggs, bouillon and garlic powder; mix well. Shape into 8 or 10 patties (about 3½ inches each), flattening centers and forming a ½-inch rim around edges. Arrange on broiler pan rack; broil 6 inches from heat 5 to 8 minutes. Meanwhile, stir together tomato paste, oregano and sugar. Spread equal portions in center of each patty. Top with your favorite toppings and cheese. Broil 1 to 2 minutes or until hot and bubbly. Serve immediately or cool completely, wrap tightly and freeze. To serve, thaw and reheat in 300° oven 15 to 20 minutes. Refrigerate leftovers.

MICROWAVE: Prepare meat patties; top with sauce and desired toppings. Arrange half the patties on a microwave roasting rack in shallow baking dish *or* on a bacon rack. Cook uncovered on 100% power (high) 7½ to 8½ minutes or to desired doneness, rotating dish once. Let stand 3 minutes before serving. Repeat with remaining patties.

LITE-LINE SANDWICH SPECIAL

Makes 4 servings
284 calories per serving

2 cups finely shredded cabbage
1 carrot, pared and shredded
3 tablespoons bottled low-calorie Italian dressing
4 slices very thin white bread, toasted
8 slices Lite-line® Process Cheese Product, any flavor*
½ pound sliced cooked lean roast beef
4 teaspoons prepared horseradish

In medium bowl, combine cabbage, carrot and dressing. On each slice of toast, place 1 Lite-line slice, equal amounts of beef, 1 teaspoon horseradish and second Lite-line slice; broil. Top with equal amounts of cabbage mixture. Refrigerate leftovers.

*"½ the calories"—8% milk fat version.

Calories by product analyses and recipe calculation.

Meatza Pizzas

EASY CHEESY ▲
MEAT LOAF

Makes 6 to 8 servings

1½ pounds lean ground beef
2 cups fresh bread crumbs (4 slices bread)
1 cup tomato juice
⅓ cup chopped onion
2 eggs
2 teaspoons Wyler's® Beef-Flavor Instant Bouillon
¼ teaspoon pepper
6 slices Borden® Process American Cheese Food

Preheat oven to 350°. In large bowl, combine all ingredients except cheese food; mix well. In shallow baking dish, shape half the mixture into loaf. Cut *4 slices* cheese food into strips; arrange on meat. Top with remaining meat; press edges together to seal. Bake 1 hour; pour off fat. Top with remaining cheese food slices. Refrigerate leftovers.

BAKED APRICOT
CHICKEN

Makes 4 to 6 servings

1 (12-ounce) jar Bama® Apricot *or* Peach Preserves (1 cup)
¼ cup ReaLemon® Lemon Juice from Concentrate
2 teaspoons soy sauce
½ teaspoon salt
1 (2½- to 3-pound) broiler-fryer chicken, cut up
1 cup dry bread crumbs
¼ cup margarine or butter, melted

Preheat oven to 350°. In shallow dish, combine preserves, ReaLemon, soy sauce and salt. Coat chicken with apricot mixture; roll in bread crumbs. Reserve remaining apricot mixture. In greased 13×9-inch baking dish, arrange chicken; drizzle with margarine. Bake uncovered 1 hour or until tender. Heat remaining apricot mixture; serve with chicken. Refrigerate leftovers.

HARVEST SAUSAGE STUFFING

Makes about 3 quarts

1 pound bulk sausage
2 cups chopped celery
8 ounces fresh mushrooms, sliced (about 2 cups)
1½ cups chopped onion
4 teaspoons Wyler's® Chicken-Flavor Instant Bouillon or 4 Chicken-Flavor Bouillon Cubes
1 to 1½ cups water
2 (7-ounce) packages herb-seasoned stuffing mix
1⅓ cups (one-half 28-ounce jar) None Such® Ready-to-Use Mincemeat
1 (8-ounce) can sliced water chestnuts, coarsely chopped
2 teaspoons poultry seasoning

In large skillet, brown sausage; pour off fat. Add celery, mushrooms and onion; cook until onion is tender. Add bouillon and water to sausage mixture; bring to a boil. In large bowl, combine remaining ingredients with sausage mixture; mix well. Use to loosely stuff turkey just before roasting; place remaining stuffing in 2-quart greased baking dish; cover. Bake at 350° for 45 minutes or until hot. Refrigerate leftovers.

SWEET AND SOUR PORK CHOPS

Makes 6 servings

6 center cut pork chops (about 1¾ pounds)
Vegetable oil
½ cup ReaLemon® Lemon Juice from Concentrate
3 tablespoons cornstarch
½ cup firmly packed brown sugar
¼ cup chopped onion
1 tablespoon soy sauce
1 teaspoon Wyler's® Chicken-Flavor Instant Bouillon or 1 Chicken-Flavor Bouillon Cube
1 (20-ounce) can pineapple chunks, drained, reserving liquid
1 cup thinly sliced carrots
Green pepper rings

Preheat oven to 350°. In large ovenproof skillet, brown chops in oil. Remove chops from skillet; pour off fat. In skillet, combine ReaLemon and cornstarch; mix well. Add sugar, onion, soy sauce, bouillon and reserved pineapple liquid; cook and stir until slightly thickened and bouillon is dissolved. Add pork chops and carrots. Cover; bake 1 hour or until tender. Add pineapple; cover and bake 10 minutes longer. Garnish with green pepper; serve with rice if desired. Refrigerate leftovers.

Harvest Sausage Stuffing

SALMON LOAF WITH CLAM CHEESE SAUCE ▶

Makes 4 to 6 servings

1 (15½-ounce) can salmon, drained and
   flaked
2 cups fresh bread crumbs (4 slices
   bread)
2 eggs
¼ cup chopped onion
3 tablespoons margarine or butter,
   melted
2 tablespoons ReaLemon® Lemon Juice
   from Concentrate
¼ teaspoon basil leaves
   Clam Cheese Sauce

Preheat oven to 350°. In large bowl, combine
all ingredients except Clam Cheese Sauce; mix
well. In greased shallow baking pan, shape
into loaf. Bake 35 to 40 minutes. Let stand 5
minutes before serving. Garnish as desired.
Serve with Clam Cheese Sauce. Refrigerate
leftovers.

Clam Cheese Sauce: Drain 1 (6½-ounce) can
Snow's® or Doxsee Minced Clams, reserving ⅓
cup liquid. In small saucepan, over low heat,
melt 1 tablespoon margarine or butter; stir in
1 tablespoon flour. Gradually stir in ⅔ cup
Borden® Milk and reserved ⅓ cup clam liquid.
Over medium heat, cook and stir until
thickened and bubbly. Remove from heat; add
¼ cup (1 ounce) shredded Cheddar cheese and
clams, stirring until cheese melts. (Makes
about 1⅓ cups)

TERIYAKI MARINADE

Makes about 1 cup

⅓ cup ReaLemon® Lemon Juice from
   Concentrate
¼ cup soy sauce
¼ cup vegetable oil
¼ cup catsup
2 tablespoons brown sugar
¼ teaspoon garlic powder
¼ teaspoon pepper

In small bowl, combine ingredients. Pour over
meat, poultry or seafood. Refrigerate 6 hours or
overnight, turning occasionally. Remove meat
from marinade; grill or broil as desired,
basting frequently with marinade.

TUNA MELT

Makes 4 sandwiches

1 (6½-ounce) can tuna, drained
⅓ cup chopped tomato
¼ cup chopped green pepper
¼ cup mayonnaise or salad dressing
8 slices bread
8 slices Borden® Process American
   Cheese Food
   Margarine or butter, softened

In medium bowl, combine tuna, tomato, pepper
and mayonnaise; spread equal amounts on 4
slices bread. Top each with 2 cheese food slices
then remaining bread slices. Spread
margarine on outside of each sandwich. Grill.
Serve immediately. Refrigerate leftovers.

BAKED MACARONI AND CHEESE

Makes 6 to 8 servings

1 (7-ounce) package *or* 2 cups uncooked Creamettes® Elbow Macaroni, cooked as package directs and drained
2 tablespoons margarine or butter
2 tablespoons flour
2 teaspoons Wyler's® Chicken-Flavor Instant Bouillon
1 teaspoon dry mustard
2½ cups Borden® Milk
2 cups (8 ounces) shredded sharp Cheddar cheese

Preheat oven to 375°. In medium saucepan, melt margarine; stir in flour, bouillon and mustard. Gradually stir in milk. Cook and stir until mixture thickens slightly (mixture should coat spoon). Remove from heat. Add *1½ cups* cheese; stir until melted. Stir in cooked macaroni. Turn into greased 1½-quart shallow baking dish. Top with remaining *½ cup* cheese. Bake 20 to 25 minutes or until bubbly. Refrigerate leftovers.

Variations: Add any of the following to macaroni before baking:

1 (6½-ounce) can tuna or salmon, drained and flaked

or

1½ cups cubed cooked chicken or turkey

or

1½ cups cubed cooked ham or luncheon meat

or

½ pound frankfurters or smoked sausage, sliced

or

1 (10-ounce) package frozen chopped broccoli or spinach, thawed and *well drained*

MICROWAVE: In 2-quart glass measure, melt margarine on 100% power (high) 1 minute. Add flour, bouillon and mustard. Gradually add milk. Cook on 100% power (high) 6 to 8 minutes or until mixture is slightly thickened, stirring every 2 minutes. Add *1½ cups* cheese; stir until melted. Add cooked macaroni. Turn into greased 1½-quart baking dish. Cook on 50% power (medium) 10 minutes. Stir; top with remaining *½ cup* cheese. Cook on 50% power (medium) 2 to 4 minutes or until cheese is melted.

SEAFOOD GUMBO ▲

Makes 6 to 8 servings

1 pound medium raw shrimp, peeled and deveined
1 cup chopped onion
¼ cup margarine or butter
3 tablespoons flour
3 cups water
1 (28-ounce) can tomatoes, undrained
½ cup chopped celery
½ cup chopped green pepper
4 teaspoons Wyler's® Chicken-Flavor Instant Bouillon *or* 4 Chicken-Flavor Bouillon Cubes
⅛ teaspoon cayenne pepper
1 (10-ounce) package frozen sliced okra
1 pint (2 cups) oysters
Hot pepper sauce, optional

In large kettle or Dutch oven, cook onion in margarine until tender; stir in flour. Cook and stir until flour is dark brown. Add remaining ingredients except okra, oysters and hot pepper sauce; bring to a boil. Simmer uncovered 1 hour. Add okra; simmer 5 minutes. Add oysters; simmer 10 minutes. Add hot pepper sauce if desired. Serve with rice. Refrigerate leftovers.

LEMON BROILED FISH ▲

Makes 4 servings

½ cup margarine or butter, melted
¼ cup ReaLemon® Lemon Juice from
   Concentrate
2 cups fresh bread crumbs (4 slices
   bread)
1 tablespoon chopped parsley
½ teaspoon paprika
1 pound fish fillets, fresh or frozen,
   thawed

Combine margarine and ReaLemon. In
medium bowl, combine bread crumbs, parsley
and ¼ *cup* of the ReaLemon mixture. Add
paprika to remaining ReaLemon mixture. Dip
fish into paprika mixture; broil until fish
flakes with fork. Top with bread crumb
mixture. Return to broiler; heat through.
Refrigerate leftovers.

B.L.T. E. BREAKFAST POCKETS

Makes 6 sandwiches

4 slices bacon, cooked and crumbled
6 eggs
⅓ cup Borden® Milk
1 teaspoon Wyler's® Chicken-Flavor
   Instant Bouillon
1 tablespoon margarine or butter
½ cup chopped tomato
3 (5-inch) pita bread rounds, cut in half
6 lettuce leaves
6 slices Borden® Process American
   Cheese Food

In medium bowl, beat eggs, milk and bouillon.
In medium skillet, melt margarine; add egg
mixture. Cook and stir until eggs are set;
remove from heat. Stir in bacon and tomato.
Fill each pita bread half with lettuce, cheese
food slice and ½ *cup* egg mixture. Serve
immediately. Refrigerate leftovers.

Preheat oven to 350°. In large saucepan, cook onion in margarine until tender. Stir in flour, salt and pepper. Gradually stir in cream and reserved clam liquid. Over medium heat, cook and stir until thickened and bubbly, about 8 minutes. Remove from heat; add noodles, clams, spinach and cheese. Mix well. Turn into greased 2-quart baking dish. Top with crumbs. Bake 25 to 30 minutes or until hot. Refrigerate leftovers.

MICROWAVE: In 3-quart round baking dish, combine onion and margarine. Cook on 100% power (high) 2 to 3 minutes or until onion is tender. Stir in flour, salt and pepper. Gradually stir in cream and reserved clam liquid. Cook on 100% power (high) 5 to 6 minutes, stirring after each minute or until thickened. Add noodles, clams, spinach and cheese; mix well. Cover tightly; cook on 70% power (medium-high) 6 to 7 minutes. Top with crumbs; cook uncovered on 70% power (medium-high) 6 to 8 minutes. Let stand 5 minutes.

SPECIAL LEMONY CHICKEN

Makes 6 servings

¼ cup unsifted flour
1 teaspoon salt
¼ teaspoon pepper
6 skinned boneless chicken breast halves
¼ cup margarine or butter
¼ cup ReaLemon® Lemon Juice from Concentrate
8 ounces fresh mushrooms, sliced (about 2 cups)
Hot cooked rice
Chopped parsley

In paper or plastic bag, combine flour, salt and pepper. Add chicken, a few pieces at a time; shake to coat. In large skillet, brown chicken in margarine on both sides until golden brown. Add ReaLemon and mushrooms. Reduce heat; cover and simmer 20 minutes or until tender. Serve with rice; garnish with parsley. Refrigerate leftovers.

CLAM NOODLE FLORENTINE ▲

Makes 6 to 8 servings

½ (1-pound) package Creamette® Egg Noodles, cooked and drained
⅓ cup chopped onion
¼ cup margarine or butter
¼ cup unsifted flour
½ teaspoon salt
¼ teaspoon pepper
2 cups (1 pint) Borden® Coffee Cream or Milk
2 (6½-ounce) cans Snow's® or Doxsee Chopped Clams, drained, reserving liquid
1 (10-ounce) package frozen chopped spinach, thawed and well drained
¼ cup grated Parmesan cheese
½ cup buttered bread crumbs

CHEESEBURGER PIE

Makes one 9-inch pie

- 1 (9-inch) unbaked pastry shell, pricked
- 8 slices Borden® Process American Cheese Food
- 1 pound lean ground beef
- ½ cup tomato sauce
- ⅓ cup chopped green pepper
- ⅓ cup chopped onion
- 1 teaspoon Wyler's® Beef-Flavor Instant Bouillon *or* 1 Beef-Flavor Bouillon Cube
- 3 eggs, well beaten
- 2 tablespoons flour
  Chopped tomato and shredded lettuce, optional

Preheat oven to 425°. Bake pastry shell 8 minutes; remove from oven. Reduce oven temperature to 350°. Cut *6 slices* cheese food into pieces; set aside. In large skillet, brown meat; pour off fat. Add tomato sauce, green pepper, onion and bouillon; cook and stir until bouillon dissolves. Remove from heat; stir in eggs, flour and cheese food pieces. Turn into prepared shell. Bake 20 to 25 minutes or until hot. Arrange remaining cheese food slices on top. Return to oven 3 to 5 minutes or until cheese food begins to melt. Garnish with tomato and lettuce if desired. Refrigerate leftovers.

MEXICAN PARTY HOAGIE

Makes 6 to 8 servings

- 1½ pounds lean ground beef
- 1 (8-ounce) can tomato sauce
- ½ cup water
- 1 (1⅛-ounce) package taco seasoning mix
- 8 slices Borden® Process American Cheese Food
- 1 (1-pound) unsliced loaf French or Italian bread (about 20 inches long)
- 1 tomato, sliced
- 1 green pepper, sliced into rings

Preheat oven to 400°. In large skillet, brown meat; pour off fat. Stir in tomato sauce, water, taco seasoning mix and *3 slices* cheese food, cut into pieces. Simmer uncovered 5 to 10 minutes, stirring occasionally. Meanwhile, cut bread in half lengthwise; scoop out center of both halves. Place bottom half of bread loaf on large piece of aluminum foil; top with meat mixture. Cut remaining *5 slices* cheese food in half diagonally; layer alternately with tomato and green pepper. Replace top of bread loaf. Tightly wrap in aluminum foil. Bake 20 minutes or until hot. Refrigerate leftovers.

Cheeseburger Pie

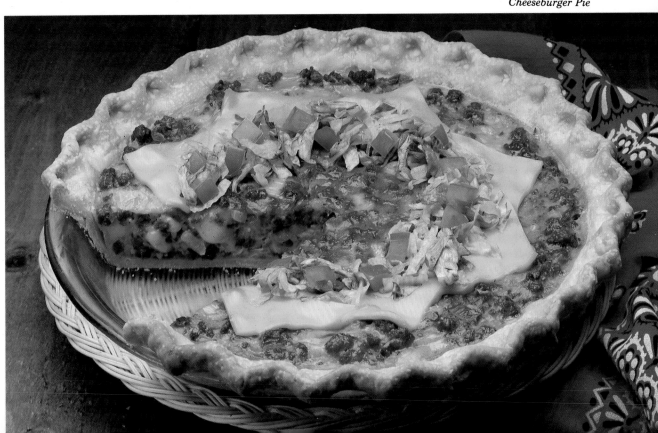

CHICKEN CASHEW ▲

Makes 4 servings

2 whole chicken breasts, split, skinned,
   boned and cut into bite-size pieces
   (about 1½ pounds)
2 teaspoons Wyler's® Chicken-Flavor
   Instant Bouillon *or* 2 Chicken-
   Flavor Bouillon Cubes
1¼ cups boiling water
2 tablespoons soy sauce
1 tablespoon cornstarch
2 teaspoons light brown sugar
½ teaspoon ground ginger
2 tablespoons vegetable oil
8 ounces fresh mushrooms, sliced
   (about 2 cups)
½ cup sliced green onions
1 small green pepper, sliced
1 (8-ounce) can sliced water chestnuts,
   drained
½ cup cashews
   Hot cooked rice

In small saucepan, dissolve bouillon in water.
Combine soy sauce, cornstarch, sugar and
ginger; stir into bouillon mixture. In large
skillet, brown chicken in oil. Add bouillon
mixture; cook and stir until slightly thickened.
Add remaining ingredients except cashews
and rice; simmer uncovered 5 to 8 minutes,
stirring occasionally. Remove from heat; add ¼
cup cashews. Serve over rice. Garnish with
remaining cashews. Refrigerate leftovers.

SOY MARINADE

Makes about 1½ cups

½ cup ReaLemon® Lemon Juice from
   Concentrate
½ cup soy sauce
½ cup vegetable oil
3 tablespoons catsup
3 to 4 cloves garlic, finely chopped
¼ teaspoon pepper

In small bowl, combine ingredients. Pour over
meat or poultry. Refrigerate 6 hours or
overnight, turning occasionally. Remove meat
from marinade; grill or broil as desired,
basting frequently with marinade.

STIR-FRIED BEEF AND VEGETABLES ▶

Makes 4 servings

1 (¾- to 1-pound) flank steak, cut diagonally into thin strips
1 large sweet onion, sliced
8 ounces fresh mushrooms, sliced (about 2 cups)
2 medium green peppers, seeded and cut into strips
1 (8-ounce) can sliced water chestnuts, drained
1 clove garlic, finely chopped
2 teaspoons Wyler's® Beef-Flavor Instant Bouillon *or* 2 Beef-Flavor Bouillon Cubes
⅓ cup water
¼ cup soy sauce
2 tablespoons cider vinegar
2½ teaspoons cornstarch
1 teaspoon sugar
¼ cup vegetable oil

In small saucepan, over low heat, dissolve bouillon in water. Combine soy sauce, vinegar, cornstarch and sugar; stir into bouillon mixture. In large heavy skillet or wok, heat *2 tablespoons* oil over high heat. Add garlic and meat; stir-fry 2 minutes (meat will be slightly pink in center). Remove meat and juices. Wipe pan; heat *1 tablespoon* oil. Add vegetables and stir-fry 2 minutes over high heat. Add remaining *1 tablespoon* oil around edge of pan; add meat and juices, then bouillon mixture. Stir; cover and cook 2 minutes. Refrigerate leftovers.

EASY PEACH GLAZE

Makes about 1 cup

1 (12-ounce) jar Bama® Peach *or* Apricot Preserves (1 cup)
2 tablespoons ReaLemon® Lemon Juice from Concentrate
1 tablespoon margarine or butter

In small saucepan, combine ingredients; bring to a boil. Reduce heat; simmer uncovered 10 to 15 minutes to blend flavors. Use to glaze ham loaf, ham, chicken, pork, carrots or sweet potatoes.

GOLDEN GLAZED HAM LOAF

Makes 8 servings

1 pound lean ground ham
1 pound ground pork
1 cup soft bread crumbs (2 slices bread)
⅓ cup chopped onion
¼ cup Borden® Milk
1 egg
Dash pepper
1 cup Bama® Peach Preserves *or*
Orange Marmalade
2 tablespoons ReaLemon® Lemon Juice
from Concentrate
1 tablespoon prepared mustard

Preheat oven to 350°. In large bowl, combine all ingredients except preserves, ReaLemon and mustard; mix well. In shallow baking dish, shape into loaf. Bake 1½ hours. Meanwhile, stir together preserves, ReaLemon and mustard. Use ⅓ to ½ cup sauce to glaze loaf during last 30 minutes of baking. Heat remaining glaze and serve with loaf. Garnish as desired. Refrigerate leftovers.

MICROWAVE: Prepare loaf as above. Cover loosely; cook on 100% power (high) 5 minutes. Rotate dish; cook on 50% power (medium) 20 to 23 minutes or until center is set. Spread with glaze as above; cook uncovered on 50% power (medium) 3 to 5 minutes. Let stand 5 minutes before serving. Meanwhile, heat remaining glaze on 100% power (high) 1 to 2 minutes or until hot, stirring after 1 minute. Serve as above.

◀ STACKED FRUIT-WICHES

Makes 2 sandwiches
224 calories each

2 slices very thin whole wheat bread
Lettuce leaves
4 slices Lite-line® Process Cheese
Product,* any flavor
1 small apple, cored and sliced
2 juice-packed pineapple slices,
drained
¼ cup Borden® Lite-line® Plain Yogurt
2 teaspoons honey
¼ teaspoon poppy seed

On each bread slice, layer lettuce, Lite-line slices, apple and pineapple. In small bowl, combine yogurt and honey; spoon over each sandwich. Sprinkle with poppy seed. Garnish as desired. Serve immediately.

*"½ the calories"—8% milk fat version.

Calories by product analyses and recipe calculation.

WILD RICE STUFFING

Makes 12 servings

1 (4-ounce) package wild rice, rinsed
and drained
4 teaspoons Wyler's® Chicken-Flavor
Instant Bouillon *or* 4 Chicken-
Flavor Bouillon Cubes
1 cup chopped celery
½ cup chopped green pepper
½ cup margarine or butter
1 cup boiling water
1 (8-ounce) package herb-seasoned
stuffing mix
2 teaspoons poultry seasoning

Prepare rice as package directs, dissolving *3 teaspoons* bouillon in water before adding rice; cook as directed. Preheat oven to 325°. In medium skillet, cook celery and green pepper in margarine until tender. Dissolve remaining *1 teaspoon* bouillon in *1 cup* water. In large bowl, combine all ingredients; mix well. Use to stuff turkey or turn into greased 2-quart baking dish; bake at 375° for 30 to 40 minutes. Refrigerate leftovers.

STUFFED FLANK STEAK

Makes 6 servings

1 (1½-pound) flank steak, pounded
2 cups herb-seasoned stuffing mix
2 teaspoons Wyler's® Beef-Flavor
    Instant Bouillon *or* 2 Beef-Flavor
    Bouillon Cubes
  Flour
3 tablespoons vegetable oil
1 cup chopped onion
1 clove garlic, chopped
2 (10¾-ounce) cans condensed tomato
    soup
½ teaspoon basil leaves
  Hot cooked noodles
  Parsley

Preheat oven to 350°. Prepare stuffing mix according to package directions, dissolving bouillon in liquid. Spread stuffing evenly on top of steak to within 1 inch of edges. Roll up, tucking in ends; tie with string. Coat roll with flour. In large skillet, brown in oil. Place in shallow baking dish. In same skillet, cook onion and garlic until tender. Add soup and basil; cook and stir until smooth. Pour over meat. Cover; bake 1 hour, basting occasionally. Serve with noodles; garnish with parsley. Refrigerate leftovers.

◄QUICK CHICKEN CURRY

Makes 6 servings

3 cups cubed cooked chicken *or* turkey
1 cup chopped onion
1 clove garlic, finely chopped
¼ cup margarine or butter
¼ cup unsifted flour
2½ cups Borden® Milk
¾ cup Coco Lopez® Cream of Coconut
1 tablespoon curry powder
1 tablespoon Wyler's® Chicken-Flavor Instant Bouillon *or* 3 Chicken-Flavor Bouillon Cubes
¼ cup ReaLemon® Lemon Juice from Concentrate
Hot cooked rice
Condiments

In large skillet, cook onion and garlic in margarine until tender; stir in flour. Gradually add milk; stir until smooth. Add cream of coconut, curry and bouillon. Over medium heat, cook and stir until thickened. Add ReaLemon; reduce heat and simmer 10 minutes. Add chicken. Cook 10 minutes longer. Serve over rice with condiments. Refrigerate leftovers.

Suggested condiments: Toasted flaked coconut, cashews, pecans or peanuts, chopped green onion, chopped hard-cooked eggs, chutney, crumbled bacon, raisins or sunflower meats.

MICROWAVE: Increase flour to *⅓ cup*; reduce milk to *2 cups*. In 2-quart round baking dish, melt margarine on 100% power (high) 45 seconds to 1 minute. Add onion and garlic. Cover; cook on 100% power (high) 4 minutes or until onion is tender. Proceed as above to add flour, milk, cream of coconut, curry and bouillon. Cook on 70% power (medium-high) 9 to 12 minutes or until slightly thickened, stirring every 2 minutes. Add ReaLemon; cook on 50% power (medium) 5 minutes. Add chicken; cook on 50% power (medium) 5 minutes or until chicken is heated through. Let stand 5 minutes before serving. Proceed as above.

VERSATILE BARBECUE SAUCE

Makes about 3 cups

2 cups catsup
½ cup firmly packed brown sugar
½ cup finely chopped onion
½ cup ReaLemon® Lemon Juice from Concentrate
¼ cup margarine or butter
¼ cup Worcestershire sauce
1 tablespoon prepared mustard
2 teaspoons Wyler's® Beef- or Chicken-Flavor Instant Bouillon *or* 2 Beef- or Chicken-Flavor Bouillon Cubes
1 clove garlic, finely chopped

In medium saucepan, combine ingredients. Simmer uncovered 20 minutes, stirring occasionally. Use as basting sauce for beef, chicken or pork. Refrigerate leftovers.

RIO GRANDE STEW ▶

Makes 8 servings

2 pounds beef cubes for stew
Flour
¼ cup vegetable oil
4½ cups water
1 (14½-ounce) can stewed tomatoes
2 medium onions, cut into wedges
2 tablespoons Wyler's® Beef-Flavor
   Instant Bouillon *or* 6 Beef-Flavor
   Bouillon Cubes
1 teaspoon ground coriander, optional
1 teaspoon ground cumin
1 teaspoon oregano leaves
¼ teaspoon garlic powder
1 bay leaf
1 cup sliced carrots
2 ears fresh or thawed frozen corn, cut
   into chunks
1 small head cabbage, cut into wedges
   (about 1 pound)
1 (4-ounce) can chopped mild green
   chilies, drained

In paper or plastic bag, add meat, a few pieces at a time, to flour; shake to coat. In large kettle or Dutch oven, brown meat in oil. Add remaining ingredients except carrots, corn, cabbage and chilies. Bring to a boil. Reduce heat; cover and simmer 1½ hours. Add remaining ingredients; cook 30 minutes longer or until vegetables are tender. Remove bay leaf. Refrigerate leftovers.

Texas-Style Chili

TEXAS-STYLE CHILI

Makes about 4 quarts

3 pounds boneless stew beef, cut into
   ½-inch cubes *or* 3 pounds lean
   ground beef
1½ cups chopped onion
1 cup chopped green pepper
3 cloves garlic, chopped
2 (28-ounce) cans tomatoes, undrained
   and broken up
2 cups water
1 (6-ounce) can tomato paste
8 teaspoons Wyler's® Beef-Flavor
   Instant Bouillon *or* 8 Beef-Flavor
   Bouillon Cubes
2 tablespoons chili powder
1 tablespoon ground cumin
2 teaspoons oregano leaves
2 teaspoons sugar

In large kettle or Dutch oven, brown beef (if using ground beef, pour off fat). Add onion, green pepper and garlic; cook and stir until tender. Add remaining ingredients. Cover; bring to a boil. Reduce heat; simmer 1½ hours (1 hour for ground beef) or until meat is tender. Serve with corn chips and shredded cheese if desired. Refrigerate leftovers.

MAIN DISHES   51

BREADS & CAKES

That tantalizing aroma wafting from the oven promises...moist, fruity muffins, nut-laden quick breads and cakes of every kind. Try our one-pan Chocolate Sheet Cake with its rich fudgy icing, or holiday fruitcake baked in a variety of shapes. You're sure to find a favorite flavor cake— carrot, lemon, apple spice, even party-special Pina Colada.

◀ GOLDEN CARROT CAKE

Makes one 10-inch cake

1 (9-ounce) package None Such® Condensed Mincemeat, crumbled
2 cups finely shredded carrots
½ cup chopped nuts
2 teaspoons grated orange rind
2 cups unsifted flour
1 cup firmly packed light brown sugar
¾ cup vegetable oil
4 eggs
2 teaspoons baking powder
1 teaspoon baking soda
1 teaspoon salt
Orange Glaze

Preheat oven to 325°. In large bowl, combine mincemeat, carrots, nuts and rind; toss with *½ cup* flour; set aside. In large mixer bowl, combine sugar and oil; mix well. Add eggs, 1 at a time, beating well after each addition. Stir together remaining *1½ cups* flour, baking powder, baking soda and salt; gradually add to batter, beating until smooth. Stir in mincemeat mixture. Turn into well-greased and floured 10-inch bundt or tube pan. Bake 50 to 60 minutes or until wooden pick comes out clean. Cool 10 minutes; remove from pan. Cool completely. Drizzle with Orange Glaze.

Orange Glaze: In small saucepan, melt 2 tablespoons margarine with 4 teaspoons orange juice. Stir in 1 cup confectioners' sugar and 1 teaspoon grated orange rind; mix well. (Makes about ½ cup)

CHOCOLATE SHEET CAKE

Makes one 15×10-inch cake

1¼ cups margarine or butter
½ cup unsweetened cocoa
1 cup water
2 cups unsifted flour
1½ cups firmly packed brown sugar
1 teaspoon baking soda
1 teaspoon ground cinnamon
½ teaspoon salt
1 (14-ounce) can Eagle® Brand Sweetened Condensed Milk (NOT evaporated milk)
2 eggs
1 teaspoon vanilla extract
1 cup confectioners' sugar
1 cup chopped nuts

Preheat oven to 350°. In small saucepan, melt *1 cup* margarine; stir in *¼ cup* cocoa then water. Bring to a boil; remove from heat. In large mixer bowl, combine flour, brown sugar, baking soda, cinnamon and salt. Add cocoa mixture; beat well. Stir in *⅓ cup* sweetened condensed milk, eggs and vanilla. Pour into greased 15×10-inch jellyroll pan. Bake 15 minutes or until cake springs back when lightly touched. In small saucepan, melt remaining *¼ cup* margarine; add remaining *¼ cup* cocoa and remaining sweetened condensed milk. Stir in confectioners' sugar and nuts. Spread on *warm* cake.

GLAZED FRUIT CRESCENTS

Makes 16 rolls

- 1 (9-ounce) package None Such® Condensed Mincemeat, crumbled
- ¼ cup orange juice
- 2 tablespoons finely chopped nuts
- ¾ teaspoon grated orange rind
- 2 (8-ounce) packages refrigerated crescent rolls
- ⅔ cup confectioners' sugar
- 4 teaspoons orange-flavored liqueur *or* orange juice
  Additional grated orange rind, optional

Preheat oven to 375°. In small saucepan, combine mincemeat and orange juice. Over medium heat, bring to a boil; cook and stir 1 minute. Add nuts and ½ *teaspoon* rind. Separate and flatten dough into 16 triangles. Spoon 1 tablespoon mincemeat mixture on shortest side of each triangle. Starting at shortest side, roll up. Place point-side down on ungreased baking sheets. Bake 12 to 15 minutes or until golden brown. Meanwhile, combine sugar, liqueur and remaining ¼ *teaspoon* rind; mix until smooth. Spoon over hot rolls; garnish with additional rind if desired. Serve warm.

Tip: To use None Such® Ready-to-Use Regular *or* Brandy & Rum Mincemeat instead of condensed mincemeat, omit orange juice. Combine 1⅓ cups ready-to-use mincemeat with nuts and rind. Omit cooking; proceed as above.

Glazed Fruit Crescents

EASY LEMON GLAZED CAKE

Makes one 10-inch cake

- 1 (18¼- to 18½-ounce) package yellow cake mix
- ⅓ cup confectioners' sugar
- ¼ cup ReaLemon® Lemon Juice from Concentrate
  Additional confectioners' sugar, optional

Preheat oven to 350°. Prepare cake mix according to package directions. Pour into greased and floured 10-inch bundt or tube pan; bake 40 minutes or until wooden pick comes out clean. While in pan, poke holes in cake 1 inch apart. In small bowl, combine sugar and ReaLemon; slowly pour half the mixture over warm cake. Let stand 10 minutes. Remove from pan; pour remaining ReaLemon mixture over cake. Cool. Sprinkle with additional confectioners' sugar if desired.

APPLE SPICE CUSTARD CAKE

Makes 8 to 10 servings

- 1 (18¼- or 18½-ounce) package spice cake mix
- 2 medium all-purpose apples, pared, cored and finely chopped (about 2 cups)
- 1 (14-ounce) can Eagle® Brand Sweetened Condensed Milk (NOT evaporated milk)
- 1 (8-ounce) container Borden® Sour Cream
- ¼ cup ReaLemon® Lemon Juice from Concentrate

Preheat oven to 350°. Prepare cake mix as package directs; stir in apples. Pour batter into well-greased and floured 13 × 9-inch baking pan. Bake 30 minutes or until wooden pick inserted near center comes out clean. Meanwhile, in medium bowl, combine sweetened condensed milk, sour cream and ReaLemon. Remove cake from oven; spread cream mixture evenly over top. Return to oven; bake 10 minutes longer or until bubbly around edges. Sprinkle with additional cinnamon. Cool. Serve warm or cooled. Store covered in refrigerator.

PUMPKIN NUT BREAD ▲

Makes two 9×5-inch loaves

3½ cups unsifted flour
2 teaspoons baking soda
1½ teaspoons ground cinnamon
½ teaspoon baking powder
2 cups sugar
⅔ cup shortening
4 eggs
1 (16-ounce) can pumpkin (about 2 cups)
½ cup water
1 (9-ounce) package None Such® Condensed Mincemeat, crumbled
1 cup chopped nuts

Preheat oven to 350°. Stir together flour, baking soda, cinnamon and baking powder; set aside. In large mixer bowl, beat sugar and shortening until fluffy. Add eggs, pumpkin and water; mix well. Stir in flour mixture, mincemeat and nuts. Turn into two greased 9×5-inch loaf pans. Bake 55 to 60 minutes or until wooden pick inserted near center comes out clean. Cool 10 minutes; remove from pans. Cool completely.

BANANA FRUIT BREAD ▲

Makes one 9×5-inch loaf

2 cups unsifted flour
1 teaspoon baking powder
½ teaspoon baking soda
¾ cup sugar
½ cup shortening
2 eggs
1 cup mashed ripe bananas (2 or 3 bananas)
½ cup Borden® Sour Cream
1 (9-ounce) package None Such® Condensed Mincemeat, crumbled

Place rack in lower half of oven; preheat oven to 350°. Stir together flour, baking powder and baking soda; set aside. In large mixer bowl, beat sugar and shortening until fluffy. Add eggs, bananas and sour cream; mix well. Stir in flour mixture and mincemeat. Turn into greased 9×5-inch loaf pan. Bake 1 hour to 1 hour and 10 minutes or until wooden pick inserted near center comes out clean. Cool 10 minutes; remove from pan. Cool completely.

Chocolate Fruitcake (left), Fruitcake-in-a-Can (center), Fruitcake Bars (right)

EVER-SO-EASY FRUITCAKE

Makes one 10-inch cake

2½ cups unsifted flour
1 teaspoon baking soda
2 eggs, slightly beaten
1 (28-ounce) jar None Such® Ready-to-Use Mincemeat (Regular *or* Brandy & Rum)
1 (14-ounce) can Eagle® Brand Sweetened Condensed Milk (NOT evaporated milk)
2 cups (1 pound) mixed candied fruit
1 cup coarsely chopped nuts

Preheat oven to 300°. Grease and flour 10-inch bundt pan. Combine flour and baking soda; set aside. In large bowl, combine remaining ingredients; blend in dry ingredients. Pour batter into prepared pan. Bake 1 hour and 45 to 50 minutes or until wooden pick comes out clean. Cool 15 minutes. Turn out of pan. Garnish as desired.

Tip: To substitute condensed mincemeat for ready-to-use mincemeat, crumble 2 (9-ounce) packages None Such® Condensed Mincemeat into small saucepan; add 1½ cups water. Boil briskly 1 minute. Cool. Proceed as above.

Chocolate Fruitcake: Prepare fruitcake batter as above, adding 3 (1-ounce) squares unsweetened chocolate, melted. For glaze, melt 3 (1-ounce) squares semi-sweet chocolate with 2 tablespoons margarine or butter. Spoon over fruitcake.

Fruitcake-in-a-Can: Grease three 1-pound coffee cans; fill each can with about 2⅔ cups batter. Bake 1 hour and 20 to 25 minutes. *Or,* grease eight 10¾-ounce soup cans; fill each with 1 cup batter. Bake 50 to 55 minutes.

Fruitcake Bars: Grease 15×10-inch jellyroll pan; spread batter evenly in pan. Bake 40 to 45 minutes. Cool. Glaze if desired. Makes about 4 dozen bars.

Fruitcake Loaves: Grease two 9×5-inch loaf pans. Pour half the batter into each pan. Bake 1 hour and 20 to 25 minutes.

Fruitcake Cookies: Drop by rounded tablespoonfuls, 2 inches apart, onto greased baking sheets. Bake 15 to 18 minutes. Makes about 5½ dozen cookies.

Fruitcake Mini Loaves: Grease twelve 4½×2½-inch loaf pans. Fill each pan ⅔ full. Bake 35 to 40 minutes.

MOIST ORANGE MINCE MUFFINS

Makes about 1½ dozen

- 2 cups unsifted flour
- ½ cup sugar
- 1 tablespoon baking powder
- 1 teaspoon salt
- ½ teaspoon baking soda
- 1 egg, slightly beaten
- 1 (8-ounce) container Borden® Lite-line® Orange Yogurt
- ⅓ cup Borden® Milk
- ⅓ cup vegetable oil
- 1 (9-ounce) package None Such® Condensed Mincemeat, finely crumbled
- ⅓ cup Bama® Orange Marmalade, melted, optional

Preheat oven to 400°. In medium bowl, combine dry ingredients; set aside. In medium bowl, combine egg, yogurt, milk, oil and mincemeat; mix well. Stir into flour mixture only until moistened. Fill greased or paper baking cup-lined muffin cups ¾ full. Bake 20 to 25 minutes or until golden brown. Immediately turn out of pan. Brush warm muffins with marmalade if desired.

CHOCOLATE SPICE SURPRISE MUFFINS

Makes about 1½ dozen

- ⅓ cup firmly packed light brown sugar
- ¼ cup margarine or butter, softened
- 1 egg
- 1 cup Borden® Milk
- 2 cups biscuit baking mix
- ⅓ cup unsweetened cocoa
- 1 (9-ounce) package None Such® Condensed Mincemeat, crumbled
- 18 solid milk chocolate candy drops
- ½ cup confectioners' sugar
- 1 tablespoon water

Preheat oven to 375°. In large mixer bowl, beat brown sugar and margarine until fluffy. Add egg and milk; mix well. Stir in biscuit mix, cocoa and mincemeat until moistened. Fill greased or paper baking cup-lined muffin cups ¾ full. Top each with candy drop; press into batter. Bake 15 to 20 minutes. Cool 5 minutes; remove from pan. Meanwhile, in small bowl, mix confectioners' sugar and water; drizzle over warm muffins.

Moist Orange Mince Muffins (left), Chocolate Spice Surprise Muffins (right)

EASY PINA COLADA CAKE

Makes one 10-inch cake

1 (18¼- to 18½-ounce) package yellow cake mix*
1 (4-serving size) package *instant* vanilla flavor pudding and pie filling mix
1 (15-ounce) can Coco Lopez® Cream of Coconut
½ cup plus 2 tablespoons rum
⅓ cup vegetable oil
4 eggs
1 (8-ounce) can crushed pineapple, *well drained*
  Whipped cream, pineapple chunks, maraschino cherries, toasted coconut for garnish

Preheat oven to 350°. In large mixer bowl, combine cake mix, pudding mix, ½ cup cream of coconut, ½ cup rum, oil and eggs. Beat on medium speed 2 minutes. Stir in pineapple. Pour into well-greased and floured 10-inch bundt or tube pan. Bake 50 to 55 minutes. Cool 10 minutes. Remove from pan. With a table knife or skewer, poke holes about 1 inch apart in cake almost to bottom. Combine remaining cream of coconut and remaining *2 tablespoons* rum; slowly spoon over cake. Chill thoroughly. Garnish. Store in refrigerator.

*If cake mix with "pudding in" is used, omit pudding mix.

Easy Pina Colada Cake

STREUSEL-TOPPED COFFEE CAKE

Makes one 9-inch cake

2¼ cups unsifted flour
2 teaspoons baking powder
½ teaspoon salt
¼ cup margarine or butter, softened
¾ cup sugar
1 egg
½ cup Borden® Milk
1⅓ cups (one-half 28-ounce jar) None Such® Ready-to-Use Mincemeat (Regular *or* Brandy & Rum)
  Streusel Topping

Preheat oven to 375°. Stir together flour, baking powder and salt; set aside. In large mixer bowl, beat margarine and sugar until fluffy; beat in egg. On low speed, add milk alternately with dry ingredients; blend well. Stir in mincemeat. Spread batter in greased 9-inch square baking pan. Sprinkle with Streusel Topping. Bake 35 to 40 minutes or until wooden pick inserted near center comes out clean. Serve warm.

Streusel Topping: In medium bowl, combine ½ cup firmly packed brown sugar, 2 tablespoons flour and 1 teaspoon ground cinnamon; cut in 2 tablespoons cold margarine until crumbly. Stir in ½ cup chopped nuts.

FUDGE RIBBON CAKE

Makes one 10-inch cake

1 (18¼- or 18½-ounce) package
    chocolate cake mix
1 (8-ounce) package cream cheese,
    softened
2 tablespoons margarine or butter,
    softened
1 tablespoon cornstarch
1 (14-ounce) can Eagle® Brand
    Sweetened Condensed Milk (NOT
    evaporated milk)
1 egg
1 teaspoon vanilla extract
    Chocolate Glaze

Preheat oven to 350°. Prepare cake mix as
package directs. Pour batter into well-greased
and floured 10-inch bundt or tube pan. In
small mixer bowl, beat cheese, margarine and
cornstarch until fluffy. Gradually beat in
sweetened condensed milk then egg and
vanilla until smooth. Pour evenly over cake
batter. Bake 50 to 55 minutes or until wooden
pick inserted near center comes out clean. Cool
10 minutes. Remove from pan. Cool
thoroughly. Top with Chocolate Glaze. Store
covered in refrigerator.

Chocolate Glaze: In small saucepan, over
low heat, melt 1 (1-ounce) square semi-sweet
chocolate and 1 tablespoon margarine or
butter with 2 tablespoons water. Remove from
heat. Stir in ¾ cup sifted confectioners' sugar
and ½ teaspoon vanilla. Stir until smooth and
well blended. (Makes about ⅓ cup)

APRICOT MINCE CONSERVE

Makes about 3 cups

1⅓ cups (one-half 28-ounce jar) None
    Such® Ready-to-Use Mincemeat
    (Regular *or* Brandy & Rum)
1 (16-ounce) jar Bama® Apricot
    Preserves
½ cup chopped walnuts, optional

In medium bowl, combine ingredients; mix
well. Store tightly covered in refrigerator.
Serve on English muffins, biscuits, rolls or
toast.

LEMON TEA MUFFINS ▲

Makes about 1½ dozen

2 cups unsifted flour
2 teaspoons baking powder
½ teaspoon salt
1 cup margarine or butter, softened
1 cup granulated sugar
4 eggs, separated
½ cup ReaLemon® Lemon Juice from
    Concentrate
¼ cup finely chopped nuts
2 tablespoons light brown sugar
¼ teaspoon ground nutmeg

Preheat oven to 375°. Stir together flour,
baking powder and salt; set aside. In large
mixer bowl, beat margarine and granulated
sugar until fluffy. Add egg yolks; beat until
light. Gradually stir in ReaLemon alternately
with dry ingredients (do not overmix). In small
mixer bowl, beat egg whites until stiff but not
dry. Fold one-third of the egg whites into
ReaLemon mixture; fold in remaining egg
whites. Fill paper baking cup-lined or greased
muffin cups ¾ full. Combine remaining
ingredients; sprinkle evenly over muffins.
Bake 15 to 20 minutes. Cool 5 minutes; remove
from pan. Serve warm.

PIES & CHEESECAKES

When it comes to the favorite American meal finale, pie or cheesecake wins hands down! From luscious fruit pies and traditional pumpkin, to lemon meringue, Fudgy Pecan and easy Cherry Cheese, there's a pie here for everyone. Or choose cheesecake! With these easy recipes, rich creamy cheesecake's not just a restaurant dessert anymore.

◄LUSCIOUS BAKED CHOCOLATE CHEESECAKE

Makes one 9-inch cheesecake

⅓ cup margarine or butter, melted
1¼ cups graham cracker crumbs
¼ cup sugar
3 (8-ounce) packages cream cheese, softened
1 (14-ounce) can Eagle® Brand Sweetened Condensed Milk (NOT evaporated milk)
1 (12-ounce) package semi-sweet chocolate chips *or* 8 (1-ounce) squares semi-sweet chocolate, melted
4 eggs
2 teaspoons vanilla extract

Preheat oven to 300°. Combine margarine, crumbs and sugar; press firmly on bottom of 9-inch springform pan. In large mixer bowl, beat cheese until fluffy. Gradually beat in sweetened condensed milk until smooth. Add remaining ingredients; mix well. Pour into prepared pan. Bake 1 hour and 5 minutes or until set. Cool. Chill thoroughly. Garnish as desired. Refrigerate leftovers.

REALEMON MERINGUE PIE

Makes one 9-inch pie

1 (9-inch) baked pastry shell
1⅔ cups sugar
6 tablespoons cornstarch
½ cup ReaLemon® Lemon Juice from Concentrate
4 eggs,* separated
1½ cups boiling water
2 tablespoons margarine or butter
¼ teaspoon cream of tartar

Preheat oven to 350°. In heavy saucepan, combine *1⅓ cups* sugar and cornstarch; add ReaLemon. In small bowl, beat egg yolks; add to ReaLemon mixture. Gradually add water, stirring constantly. Over medium heat, cook and stir until mixture boils and thickens, about 8 to 10 minutes. Remove from heat. Add margarine; stir until melted. Pour into prepared pastry shell. In small mixer bowl, beat egg whites with cream of tartar until soft peaks form; gradually add remaining *⅓ cup* sugar, beating until stiff but not dry. Spread on top of pie, sealing carefully to edge of shell. Bake 12 to 15 minutes or until golden brown. Cool. Chill before serving. Refrigerate leftovers.

*Use only Grade A clean, uncracked eggs.

TRADITIONAL PUMPKIN PIE

Makes one 9-inch pie

- 1 (9-inch) unbaked pastry shell
- 1 (16-ounce) can pumpkin (about 2 cups)
- 1 (14-ounce) can Eagle® Brand Sweetened Condensed Milk (NOT evaporated milk)
- 2 eggs
- 1 teaspoon ground cinnamon
- ½ teaspoon ground ginger
- ½ teaspoon ground nutmeg
- ½ teaspoon salt

Preheat oven to 425°. In large mixer bowl, combine all ingredients except pastry shell; mix well. Pour into pastry shell. Bake 15 minutes. Reduce oven temperature to 350°; continue baking 35 to 40 minutes or until knife inserted 1 inch from edge comes out clean. Cool. Garnish as desired. Refrigerate leftovers.

Sour Cream Topping: In medium bowl, combine 1½ cups Borden® Sour Cream, 2 tablespoons sugar and 1 teaspoon vanilla extract. After 30 minutes of baking, spread evenly over top of pie; bake 10 minutes longer. Garnish as desired.

Streusel Topping: In medium bowl, combine ½ cup firmly packed light brown sugar and ½ cup unsifted flour; cut in ¼ cup cold margarine or butter until crumbly. Stir in ¼ cup chopped nuts. After 30 minutes of baking, sprinkle on top of pie; bake 10 minutes longer.

◀ CREAMY LEMON PIE

Makes one 8- or 9-inch pie

- 1 (8- or 9-inch) graham cracker crumb crust
- 3 egg yolks*
- 1 (14-ounce) can Eagle® Brand Sweetened Condensed Milk (NOT evaporated milk)
- ½ cup ReaLemon® Lemon Juice from Concentrate
  Few drops yellow food coloring, optional
  Whipped topping or whipped cream

In medium bowl, beat egg yolks; stir in sweetened condensed milk, ReaLemon and food coloring if desired. Pour into prepared crust. Chill 4 hours or until set. Top with whipped topping. Garnish as desired. Refrigerate leftovers.

Creamy Lemon Meringue Pie: Omit whipped topping. In small mixer bowl, beat 3 egg whites with ¼ teaspoon cream of tartar until soft peaks form; gradually add ⅓ cup sugar, beating until stiff but not dry. Spread on top of pie, sealing carefully to edge of crust. Bake in preheated 350° oven 12 to 15 minutes or until golden brown. Cool. Chill thoroughly.

Raspberry Topped Lemon Pie: Prepare lemon filling as above. Pour into crust. In small saucepan, over medium heat, combine 1 (10-ounce) package frozen red raspberries in syrup, thawed, and 1 tablespoon cornstarch; cook and stir until mixture thickens and is clear. Cool 15 minutes. Spoon evenly over lemon filling. Chill 4 hours or until set. Top with whipped topping. Garnish as desired.

*Use only Grade A clean, uncracked eggs.

Traditional Pumpkin Pie

FROZEN PEANUT BUTTER PIE ▲

Makes one 9- or 10-inch pie

Chocolate Crunch Crust
1 (8-ounce) package cream cheese, softened
1 (14-ounce) can Eagle® Brand Sweetened Condensed Milk (NOT evaporated milk)
¾ cup peanut butter
2 tablespoons ReaLemon® Lemon Juice from Concentrate
1 teaspoon vanilla extract
1 cup (½ pint) Borden® Whipping Cream, whipped
Chocolate fudge ice cream topping

Prepare crust. In large mixer bowl, beat cheese until fluffy; gradually beat in sweetened condensed milk then peanut butter until smooth. Stir in ReaLemon and vanilla. Fold in whipped cream. Turn into prepared crust. Drizzle chocolate topping over pie. Freeze 4 hours or until firm. Return leftovers to freezer.

Chocolate Crunch Crust: In heavy saucepan, over low heat, melt ⅓ cup margarine or butter and 1 (6-ounce) package semi-sweet chocolate chips. Remove from heat; gently stir in 2½ cups oven-toasted rice cereal until completely coated. Press on bottom and up side to rim of buttered 9- or 10-inch pie plate. Chill 30 minutes.

STREUSEL-TOPPED APPLE CUSTARD PIE

Makes one 9-inch pie

1 (9-inch) unbaked pastry shell
4 large all-purpose apples, pared and sliced (about 4 cups)
2 eggs
1 (14-ounce) can Eagle® Brand Sweetened Condensed Milk (NOT evaporated milk)
¼ cup margarine or butter, melted
½ teaspoon ground cinnamon
  Dash ground nutmeg
½ cup firmly packed light brown sugar
½ cup unsifted flour
¼ cup cold margarine or butter
¼ cup chopped nuts

Preheat oven to 425°. Arrange apples in pastry shell. In medium bowl, beat eggs. Add sweetened condensed milk, melted margarine, cinnamon and nutmeg; mix well. Pour over apples. In medium bowl, combine sugar and flour; cut in cold margarine until crumbly. Stir in nuts. Sprinkle over pie. Place in bottom third of oven; bake 10 minutes. Reduce oven temperature to 375°; continue baking 35 to 40 minutes or until golden brown. Cool. Refrigerate leftovers.

Peach Variation: Omit apples. Substitute 1 (29-ounce) can sliced peaches, well drained, for apples. Proceed as above.

CREAMY FRUIT & NUT CHEESECAKE ▲

Makes one 9-inch cheesecake

⅓ cup margarine or butter, melted
1¼ cups graham cracker crumbs
¼ cup sugar
2 (8-ounce) packages cream cheese, softened
1 (14-ounce) can Eagle® Brand Sweetened Condensed Milk (NOT evaporated milk)
1 envelope unflavored gelatine
¼ cup ReaLemon® Lemon Juice from Concentrate
1⅓ cups (one-half 28-ounce jar) None Such® Ready-to-Use Mincemeat (Regular *or* Brandy & Rum)
½ cup chopped nuts
1 tablespoon grated lemon rind
1 cup (½ pint) Borden® Whipping Cream, whipped
Sour cream and nuts, optional

Combine margarine, crumbs and sugar; press firmly on bottom of 9-inch springform *or* 9-inch square baking pan. In large mixer bowl, beat cheese until fluffy. Gradually beat in sweetened condensed milk until smooth. In small saucepan, sprinkle gelatine over ReaLemon; let stand 1 minute. Over low heat, stir until gelatine dissolves. Add to cheese mixture with mincemeat, ½ *cup* nuts and rind; mix well. Fold in whipped cream. Pour into prepared pan. Chill 3 hours or until set. Garnish with sour cream and additional nuts if desired. Refrigerate leftovers.

FROZEN PEPPERMINT CHEESECAKE

Makes one 9-inch cheesecake

1¼ cups chocolate wafer cookie crumbs (about 24 wafers)
¼ cup margarine or butter, melted
¼ cup sugar
1 (8-ounce) package cream cheese, softened
1 (14-ounce) can Eagle® Brand Sweetened Condensed Milk (NOT evaporated milk)
1 cup crushed hard peppermint candy
½ cup mini chocolate chips, optional
Few drops red food coloring, optional
2 cups (1 pint) Borden® Whipping Cream, whipped
Additional hard peppermint candies, optional

Combine crumbs, margarine and sugar; press firmly on bottom and halfway up side of 9-inch springform pan *or* 13×9-inch baking dish. In large mixer bowl, beat cheese until fluffy. Gradually beat in sweetened condensed milk. Stir in crushed candy, chips and food coloring if desired. Fold in whipped cream. Pour into prepared pan; cover. Freeze 6 hours or overnight. Garnish with peppermint candies if desired. Return leftovers to freezer.

FLUFFY YOGURT FRUIT PIE

Makes one 9-inch pie

- 1 (9-inch) graham cracker crumb crust
- 1 (8-ounce) package cream cheese, softened
- 1 (14-ounce) can Eagle® Brand Sweetened Condensed Milk (NOT evaporated milk)
- 1 (8-ounce) container Borden® Lite-line® Strawberry or other Fruit Yogurt
- 2 tablespoons ReaLemon® Lemon Juice from Concentrate
- 2 to 3 drops red or other food coloring, optional
- 1 (8-ounce) container frozen non-dairy whipped topping, thawed
  Strawberries or other fresh fruit

In large mixer bowl, beat cheese until fluffy. Gradually beat in sweetened condensed milk until smooth. Stir in remaining ingredients except crust, whipped topping and strawberries. Fold in whipped topping. Pour into prepared crust. Garnish with strawberries. Chill 4 hours or overnight until set. Refrigerate leftovers.

WALNUT MINCE PIE

Makes one 9-inch pie

- 1 (9-inch) unbaked pastry shell
- ½ cup sugar
- 2 tablespoons flour
- ⅛ teaspoon salt
- 2 eggs, slightly beaten
- 2 tablespoons margarine or butter, melted
- 1 cup chopped walnuts
- 1 (28-ounce) jar None Such® Ready-to-Use Mincemeat (Regular or Brandy & Rum)

Preheat oven to 400°. In large bowl, combine sugar, flour and salt. Add eggs; mix well. Add margarine, walnuts and mincemeat; mix well. Turn into pastry shell. Bake 15 minutes. Reduce oven temperature to 325°; bake 50 minutes longer or until filling is slightly puffed and firm. Cool slightly. Serve warm or cool. Garnish with whipped cream if desired.

BUTTERSCOTCH CHEESECAKE

Makes one 9-inch cheesecake

- ⅓ cup margarine or butter, melted
- 1½ cups graham cracker crumbs
- ⅓ cup firmly packed brown sugar
- 1 (14-ounce) can Eagle® Brand Sweetened Condensed Milk (NOT evaporated milk)
- ¾ cup cold water
- 1 (4-serving size) package butterscotch flavor pudding and pie filling mix
- 3 (8-ounce) packages cream cheese, softened
- 3 eggs
- 1 teaspoon vanilla extract
  Whipped cream
  Crushed hard butterscotch candy

Preheat oven to 375°. Combine margarine, crumbs and sugar; press firmly on bottom of 9-inch springform pan. In medium saucepan, combine sweetened condensed milk and water; mix well. Stir in pudding mix. Over medium heat, cook and stir until thickened and bubbly. In large mixer bowl, beat cheese until fluffy. Beat in eggs and vanilla then pudding mixture. Pour into prepared pan. Bake 50 minutes or until golden brown around edge (center will be soft). Cool to room temperature. Chill thoroughly. Garnish with whipped cream and crushed candy. Refrigerate leftovers.

Butterscotch Cheesecake

CARAMEL DATE CREAM PIE (MICROWAVE)

Makes 1 pie

- 1 (14-ounce) can Eagle® Brand Sweetened Condensed Milk (NOT evaporated milk)
- ⅔ cup chopped dates
- ⅔ cup chopped pecans
- 2 tablespoons Borden® Milk
- 1 cup (½ pint) Borden® Whipping Cream, whipped
- 1 (6-ounce) packaged graham cracker crumb crust

Pour sweetened condensed milk into 2-quart glass measure. Cook on 50% power (medium) 4 minutes, stirring after 2 minutes. Reduce to 20% power (low); cook 12 to 18 minutes or until thick and light caramel-colored, stirring briskly every 2 minutes until smooth. Stir in dates, pecans and milk; cool. Chill thoroughly. Fold in whipped cream. Pour into crust. Chill 3 hours or until set. Garnish as desired. Refrigerate leftovers.

CAUTION: NEVER HEAT UNOPENED CAN OF EAGLE® BRAND SWEETENED CONDENSED MILK.

Apple Walnut Upside-Down Pie

APPLE WALNUT UPSIDE-DOWN PIE

Makes one 9-inch pie

- Pastry for 2-crust pie
- ¼ cup firmly packed light brown sugar
- 2 tablespoons margarine or butter, melted
- ½ cup chopped walnuts
- 4 cups pared and sliced all-purpose apples (about 2 pounds)
- ⅔ to 1 cup granulated sugar
- 2 to 3 tablespoons flour
- 2 tablespoons ReaLemon® Lemon Juice from Concentrate
- 1 teaspoon ground cinnamon

Preheat oven to 400°. In 9-inch pie plate, combine brown sugar and margarine; spread over bottom. Sprinkle nuts evenly over sugar mixture. Divide pastry in half; roll each into 12-inch circle. Carefully line prepared pie plate with 1 pastry circle; *do not press* into nut mixture. Trim pastry even with edge of plate. Combine remaining ingredients; turn into prepared pastry shell. Cover with remaining pastry circle; prick with fork. Trim top crust even with edge of plate; seal crust edges with water. Roll edges *toward center* of pie (crust edge should *not* touch rim of plate). Place aluminum foil or baking sheet on bottom oven rack to catch drippings. Bake 40 to 45 minutes or until golden brown. Let stand 2 minutes; carefully run knife tip around edge of pie plate to loosen pie. Invert onto serving plate. Serve warm with ice cream if desired.

CRUMB CRUST

Makes one 8- or 9-inch crust

- 1½ cups graham cracker or chocolate wafer crumbs
- ¼ cup sugar
- 6 tablespoons margarine or butter, melted

Combine ingredients; mix well. Press firmly on bottom and up side to rim of 8- or 9-inch pie plate. Chill thoroughly or bake in preheated 375° oven 6 to 8 minutes or until edges are brown. Cool before filling.

CHERRY CHEESE PIE ▲

Makes one 9-inch pie

1 (9-inch) graham cracker crumb crust
  or baked pastry shell
1 (8-ounce) package cream cheese,
  softened
1 (14-ounce) can Eagle® Brand
  Sweetened Condensed Milk (NOT
  evaporated milk)
⅓ cup ReaLemon® Lemon Juice from
  Concentrate
1 teaspoon vanilla extract
1 (21-ounce) can cherry pie filling,
  chilled

In large mixer bowl, beat cheese until fluffy.
Gradually beat in sweetened condensed milk
until smooth. Stir in ReaLemon and vanilla.
Pour into prepared pastry shell. Chill 3 hours
or until set. Top with desired amount of pie
filling before serving. Refrigerate leftovers.

Ambrosia Topping: Omit cherry pie filling.
In small saucepan, combine ½ cup Bama®
Peach *or* Apricot Preserves, ¼ cup flaked
coconut, 2 tablespoons orange juice *or* orange-
flavored liqueur and 2 teaspoons cornstarch;
cook and stir until thickened. Remove from
heat. Arrange fresh orange sections over top of
pie; top with coconut mixture. Chill
thoroughly.

EASY KEY LIME PIE

Makes one pie

3 egg yolks*
1 (14-ounce) can Eagle® Brand
  Sweetened Condensed Milk (NOT
  evaporated milk)
½ cup ReaLime® Lime Juice from
  Concentrate
  Few drops green food coloring,
  optional
1 (6-ounce) packaged graham cracker
  crumb crust
  Whipped topping or whipped cream

In medium bowl, beat egg yolks; stir in
sweetened condensed milk, ReaLime and food
coloring if desired. Pour into crust. Chill 4
hours or until set. Top with whipped topping.
Garnish as desired. Refrigerate leftovers.

Key Lime Meringue Pie: Omit whipped
topping. In small mixer bowl, beat 3 egg whites
with ¼ teaspoon cream of tartar until soft
peaks form; gradually add ⅓ cup sugar,
beating until stiff but not dry. Spread on top of
pie, sealing carefully to edge of crust. Bake in
preheated 350° oven 12 to 15 minutes or until
golden brown. Cool. Chill thoroughly.

*Use only Grade A clean, uncracked eggs.

PEACHY MINCE PIE WITH CHEDDAR CRUST ▲

Makes one 9-inch pie

- 1 (9-ounce) package pie crust mix
- 1 cup (4 ounces) shredded sharp Cheddar cheese
- 1 (28-ounce) jar None Such® Ready-to-Use Mincemeat (Regular *or* Brandy & Rum)
- 1 (16-ounce) can sliced peaches, drained
- 1 egg yolk plus 2 tablespoons water, optional

Place rack in lower half of oven; preheat oven to 425°. Prepare pie crust mix as package directs for 2-crust pie, adding cheese. Turn mincemeat into pastry-lined 9-inch pie plate. Top with peach slices. Cover with top crust; cut slits near center. Seal and flute. For a more golden crust, mix egg yolk and water; brush over entire surface of pie. Bake 20 minutes or until golden. Serve warm or cool. Garnish as desired.

HARVEST CHERRY PIE ▲

Makes one 9-inch pie

- Pastry for 2-crust pie
- 1⅓ cups (one-half 28-ounce jar) None Such® Ready-to-Use Mincemeat (Regular *or* Brandy & Rum)
- ¾ cup chopped nuts
- 1 (21-ounce) can cherry pie filling
- 1 egg yolk plus 2 tablespoons water, optional

Place rack in lower half of oven; preheat oven to 425°. In small bowl, stir together mincemeat and nuts; turn into pastry-lined 9-inch pie plate. Spoon cherry pie filling over mincemeat. Cover with top crust; cut slits near center. Seal and flute. For a more golden crust, mix egg yolk and water; brush over entire surface of pie. Bake 25 to 30 minutes or until golden brown. Serve warm or cool. Garnish as desired.

BANANA CREAM CHEESE PIE ▶

Makes one 9-inch pie

1 (9-inch) graham cracker crumb crust
   or baked pastry shell
1 (8-ounce) package cream cheese,
   softened
1 (14-ounce) can Eagle® Brand
   Sweetened Condensed Milk (NOT
   evaporated milk)
⅓ cup ReaLemon® Lemon Juice from
   Concentrate
1 teaspoon vanilla extract
3 to 4 medium bananas, sliced and
   dipped in additional ReaLemon and
   drained

In large mixer bowl, beat cheese until fluffy.
Gradually beat in sweetened condensed milk
until smooth. Stir in ReaLemon and vanilla.
Line crust with *2 bananas*. Pour filling over
bananas; cover. Chill 3 hours or until set. Just
before serving, arrange remaining banana
slices on top of pie. Refrigerate leftovers.

Chocolate Chip Cheesecake

CHOCOLATE CHIP CHEESECAKE

Makes one 9-inch cheesecake

1½ cups finely crushed creme-filled
   chocolate sandwich cookies (about
   18 cookies)
2 to 3 tablespoons margarine or butter,
   melted
3 (8-ounce) packages cream cheese,
   softened
1 (14-ounce) can Eagle® Brand
   Sweetened Condensed Milk (NOT
   evaporated milk)
3 eggs
2 teaspoons vanilla extract
1 cup mini chocolate chips
1 teaspoon flour

Preheat oven to 300°. Combine crushed cookies
and margarine; press firmly on bottom of
9-inch springform pan *or* 13×9-inch baking
pan. In large mixer bowl, beat cheese until
fluffy. Gradually beat in sweetened condensed
milk until smooth. Add eggs and vanilla; mix
well. In small bowl, toss together *½ cup* chips
with flour to coat; stir into cheese mixture.
Pour into prepared pan. Sprinkle remaining
chips evenly over top. Bake 55 to 60 minutes or
until set. Cool. Chill thoroughly. Garnish as
desired. Refrigerate leftovers.

Mint Chocolate Chip Cheesecake: Omit
vanilla. Add ½ to 1 teaspoon peppermint
extract and ⅛ to ¼ teaspoon green food
coloring if desired.

FUDGY PECAN PIE

Makes one 9-inch pie

1 (9-inch) unbaked pastry shell
1 (4-ounce) package sweet cooking
  chocolate *or* 2 (1-ounce) squares
  unsweetened chocolate
¼ cup margarine or butter
1 (14-ounce) can Eagle® Brand
  Sweetened Condensed Milk (NOT
  evaporated milk)
½ cup hot water
2 eggs, well beaten
1 teaspoon vanilla extract
⅛ teaspoon salt
1¼ cups pecan halves or pieces

Preheat oven 350°. In medium saucepan, over low heat, melt chocolate with margarine. Stir in sweetened condensed milk, hot water and eggs; *mix well*. Remove from heat; stir in vanilla, salt and pecans. Pour into pastry shell. Bake 40 to 45 minutes or until center is set. Cool slightly. Serve warm or chilled. Garnish as desired. Refrigerate leftovers.

ALMOND CHEESECAKE ▲

Makes one 9-inch cheesecake

¾ cup graham cracker crumbs
½ cup slivered almonds, toasted and
  finely chopped
¼ cup sugar
¼ cup margarine or butter, melted
3 (8-ounce) packages cream cheese,
  softened
1 (14-ounce) can Eagle® Brand
  Sweetened Condensed Milk (NOT
  evaporated milk)
3 eggs
1 teaspoon almond extract
  Almond Praline Topping

Preheat oven to 300°. Combine crumbs, almonds, sugar and margarine; press firmly on bottom of 9-inch springform pan *or* 13×9-inch baking pan. In large mixer bowl, beat cheese until fluffy. Gradually beat in sweetened condensed milk until smooth. Add eggs and extract; mix well. Pour into prepared pan. Bake 55 to 60 minutes or until set. Cool. Top with Almond Praline Topping. Chill thoroughly. Refrigerate leftovers.

Almond Praline Topping: In small saucepan, combine ⅓ cup firmly packed dark brown sugar and ⅓ cup Borden® Whipping Cream. Cook and stir until sugar dissolves. Simmer 5 minutes. Remove from heat; stir in ½ cup chopped toasted slivered almonds. Spoon evenly over cake. (For 13×9-inch pan, double all topping ingredients; simmer 10 to 12 minutes.)

NO-BAKE PUMPKIN PIE

Makes one pie

1 egg
1 (14-ounce) can Eagle® Brand
  Sweetened Condensed Milk (NOT
  evaporated milk)
1 teaspoon ground cinnamon
½ teaspoon *each* ground ginger, nutmeg
  and salt
1 envelope unflavored gelatine
2 tablespoons water
1 (16-ounce) can pumpkin (about 2
  cups)
1 (6-ounce) packaged graham cracker
  crumb crust

In medium bowl, beat egg; beat in sweetened condensed milk and spices. In medium saucepan, sprinkle gelatine over water; let stand 1 minute. Over *low* heat, stir until gelatine dissolves. Add sweetened condensed milk mixture; over *low* heat, cook and stir constantly until mixture thickens slightly, 5 to 10 minutes. Remove from heat. Add pumpkin. Pour into crust. Chill 4 hours or until set. Garnish as desired. Refrigerate leftovers.

ORANGE CHEESECAKE

Makes one 9-inch cheesecake

1½ cups vanilla wafer crumbs (about 45 wafers)
¼ cup margarine or butter, melted
3 (8-ounce) packages cream cheese, softened
1 (14-ounce) can Eagle® Brand Sweetened Condensed Milk (NOT evaporated milk)
¼ cup frozen orange juice concentrate, thawed
3 eggs
1 teaspoon grated orange rind
Fresh orange sections
Orange Glaze

Preheat oven to 300°. Combine crumbs and margarine; press firmly on bottom of 9-inch springform pan *or* 13×9-inch baking pan. In large mixer bowl, beat cheese until fluffy. Gradually beat in sweetened condensed milk until smooth. Add juice concentrate, eggs and rind; mix well. Pour into prepared pan. Bake 55 to 60 minutes or until set. Cool. Top with orange sections then Orange Glaze. Chill thoroughly. Refrigerate leftovers.

Orange Glaze: In small saucepan, combine ¼ cup sugar and 2 teaspoons cornstarch. Add ½ cup orange juice and ¼ teaspoon grated orange rind; mix well. Over medium heat, cook and stir until thickened. Remove from heat; cool slightly. (For 13×9-inch pan, double all topping ingredients.)

Orange Cheesecake

CRANBERRY CRUMB PIE

Makes one 9-inch pie

1 (9-inch) unbaked pastry shell
1 (8-ounce) package cream cheese, softened
1 (14-ounce) can Eagle® Brand Sweetened Condensed Milk (NOT evaporated milk)
¼ cup ReaLemon® Lemon Juice from Concentrate
3 tablespoons light brown sugar
2 tablespoons cornstarch
1 (16-ounce) can whole berry cranberry sauce
¼ cup cold margarine or butter
⅓ cup unsifted flour
¾ cup chopped walnuts

Preheat oven to 425°. Bake pastry shell 8 minutes; remove from oven. Reduce oven temperature to 375°. In large mixer bowl, beat cheese until fluffy. Gradually beat in sweetened condensed milk until smooth. Stir in ReaLemon. Pour into prepared pastry shell. In small bowl, combine *1 tablespoon* sugar and cornstarch; mix well. Stir in cranberry sauce. Spoon evenly over cheese mixture. In medium bowl, cut margarine into flour and remaining *2 tablespoons* sugar until crumbly. Stir in nuts. Sprinkle evenly over cranberry mixture. Bake 45 to 50 minutes or until bubbly and golden. Cool. Serve at room temperature or chill thoroughly. Refrigerate leftovers.

CREAMY BAKED CHEESECAKE

Makes one 9-inch cheesecake

- ⅓ cup margarine or butter, melted
- 1¼ cups graham cracker crumbs
- ¼ cup sugar
- 2 (8-ounce) packages cream cheese, softened
- 1 (14-ounce) can Eagle® Brand Sweetened Condensed Milk (NOT evaporated milk)
- 3 eggs
- ¼ cup ReaLemon® Lemon Juice from Concentrate
- 1 (8-ounce) container Borden® Sour Cream
- Peach Melba Topping, optional

Preheat oven to 300°. Combine margarine, crumbs and sugar; press firmly on bottom of 9-inch springform pan. In large mixer bowl, beat cheese until fluffy. Gradually beat in sweetened condensed milk until smooth. Add eggs and ReaLemon; mix well. Pour into prepared pan. Bake 50 to 55 minutes or until set. Cool. Chill thoroughly. Spread sour cream on top. Serve with Peach Melba Topping if desired. Refrigerate leftovers.

Peach Melba Topping: Reserve ⅔ cup syrup drained from 1 (10-ounce) package thawed frozen red raspberries. In small saucepan, combine reserved syrup, ¼ cup red currant jelly and 1 tablespoon cornstarch. Cook and stir until slightly thickened and clear. Cool. Stir in raspberries. Drain 1 (16-ounce) can peach slices; arrange on cake. Top with sauce.

New York Style Cheesecake: Prepare crust. Omit sour cream. Preheat oven to 350°. Beat 4 (8-ounce) packages cream cheese until fluffy. Gradually add sweetened condensed milk; beat until smooth. Add 4 eggs, ¼ cup ReaLemon and 2 tablespoons flour; mix well. Pour into prepared pan. Bake 1 hour or until lightly browned. Cool. Chill thoroughly.

CREAMY CHOCOLATE PIE

Makes one 9-inch pie

1 (9-inch) baked pastry shell
3 (1-ounce) squares unsweetened *or*
 semi-sweet chocolate
1 (14-ounce) can Eagle® Brand
 Sweetened Condensed Milk (NOT
 evaporated milk)
¼ teaspoon salt
¼ cup hot water
1 teaspoon vanilla extract
1 cup (½ pint) Borden® Whipping
 Cream
 Additional whipped cream and
 shaved chocolate

In heavy saucepan, over medium heat, melt chocolate with sweetened condensed milk and salt. Cook and stir until very thick and fudgy, 5 to 8 minutes. Add water; cook and stir until mixture thickens and bubbles. Remove from heat; stir in vanilla. Cool 15 minutes. Chill thoroughly, 20 to 30 minutes; stir. In large mixer bowl, beat *1 cup* whipping cream until stiff; fold in cooled chocolate mixture. Pour into prepared pastry shell. Chill 3 hours or until set. Garnish with additional whipped cream and shaved chocolate. Refrigerate leftovers.

Creamy Chocolate Pie

APPLE STREUSEL MINCE PIE ▲

Makes one 9-inch pie

1 (9-inch) unbaked pastry shell
3 all-purpose apples, pared and thinly
 sliced
½ cup plus 3 tablespoons unsifted flour
2 tablespoons margarine or butter,
 melted
1 (28-ounce) jar None Such® Ready-to-
 Use Mincemeat (Regular *or* Brandy
 & Rum)
¼ cup firmly packed light brown sugar
1 teaspoon ground cinnamon
⅓ cup cold margarine or butter
¼ cup chopped nuts

Preheat oven to 425°. In large bowl, toss apples with *3 tablespoons* flour and melted margarine; arrange in pastry shell. Top with mincemeat. In medium bowl, combine remaining *½ cup* flour, sugar and cinnamon; cut in cold margarine until crumbly. Stir in nuts. Sprinkle over mincemeat. Bake 10 minutes. Reduce oven temperature to 375°; continue baking 25 to 30 minutes or until golden brown. Cool slightly. Serve warm. Garnish as desired.

DESSERTS

No meal's complete without dessert! From simple to sensational, these recipes include extra creamy puddings, rich dessert sauces, easy homemade ice creams—without an ice cream maker—and luscious fruit desserts. For that special occasion, make a classic dessert like Caramel Flan or chocolate mousse.

HOT FUDGE SAUCE

Makes about 2 cups

1 (6-ounce) package semi-sweet chocolate chips *or* 4 (1-ounce) squares semi-sweet chocolate
2 tablespoons margarine or butter
1 (14-ounce) can Eagle® Brand Sweetened Condensed Milk (NOT evaporated milk)
2 tablespoons water
1 teaspoon vanilla extract

In heavy saucepan, over medium heat, melt chips and margarine with sweetened condensed milk, water and vanilla. Cook and stir constantly until thickened, about 5 minutes. Serve warm over ice cream. Refrigerate leftovers.

To Reheat: In small heavy saucepan, combine desired amount of sauce with small amount of water. Over low heat, stir constantly until heated through.

MICROWAVE: In 1-quart glass measure, combine ingredients. Cook on 100% power (high) 1½ minutes; mix well. Cook on 100% power (high) 2 to 2½ minutes, stirring after each minute.

Variations:

Mocha: Add 1 teaspoon instant coffee. Proceed as above.

Spirited: Add ⅓ cup almond, coffee, mint *or* orange-flavored liqueur after mixture has thickened.

Mexican: Omit water. Add 2 tablespoons coffee-flavored liqueur *or* 1 teaspoon instant coffee dissolved in 2 tablespoons water and 1 teaspoon ground cinnamon after mixture has thickened.

Chocolate Peanut Butter: Increase water to ¼ cup. Add ½ cup creamy peanut butter. Proceed as above.

FROZEN CHOCOLATE BANANA LOAF

Makes 8 to 10 servings

1½ cups chocolate wafer cookie crumbs (about 30 wafers)
¼ cup sugar
3 tablespoons margarine or butter, melted
1 (14-ounce) can Eagle® Brand Sweetened Condensed Milk (NOT evaporated milk)
⅔ cup chocolate flavored syrup
2 small ripe bananas, mashed (¾ cup)
2 cups (1 pint) Borden® Whipping Cream, whipped (*do not use non-dairy whipped topping*)

Line 9×5-inch loaf pan with aluminum foil, extending foil above sides of pan; butter foil. Combine crumbs, sugar and margarine; press firmly on bottom and halfway up sides of prepared pan. In large bowl, combine sweetened condensed milk, syrup and bananas; mix well. Fold in whipped cream. Pour into prepared pan; cover. Freeze 6 hours or until firm. To serve, remove from pan; peel off foil. Garnish as desired; slice. Return leftovers to freezer.

Frozen Chocolate Banana Loaf

BANANAS COCO LOPEZ ▲

Makes 4 to 6 servings

4 firm medium bananas, peeled and
 sliced
 ReaLemon® Lemon Juice from
 Concentrate
1 cup Coco Lopez® Cream of Coconut
¼ teaspoon ground cinnamon
½ teaspoon vanilla extract

Dip bananas in ReaLemon. In large skillet or
chafing dish, combine cream of coconut and
cinnamon; bring to a boil. Add bananas and
vanilla. Over medium heat, cook and stir 2 to 3
minutes. Serve warm over ice cream or cake.

MICROWAVE: Dip bananas in ReaLemon. In
2-quart glass measure, combine cream of
coconut and cinnamon. Cook on 100% power
(high) 2 minutes or until mixture boils. Add
bananas and vanilla. Cook on 100% power
(high) 1½ to 2 minutes or until bananas are
heated through (do not overheat).

COCONUT FUDGE SAUCE ▲

Makes about 3½ cups

1 (6-ounce) package semi-sweet
 chocolate chips or 4 (1-ounce)
 squares semi-sweet chocolate
1 (14-ounce) can Eagle® Brand
 Sweetened Condensed Milk (NOT
 evaporated milk)
1 (15-ounce) can Coco Lopez® Cream of
 Coconut

In heavy saucepan, over medium heat, melt
chips with sweetened condensed milk. Cook,
stirring constantly, until sauce is slightly
thickened, about 5 minutes. Gradually stir in
cream of coconut; heat through. Serve warm
over ice cream or with fresh fruit. Refrigerate
leftovers.

MICROWAVE: In 1-quart glass measure,
combine chips and sweetened condensed milk.
Cook on 100% power (high) 3 to 3½ minutes,
stirring after each minute. Gradually stir in
cream of coconut; cook on 100% power (high) 2
minutes, stirring after each minute.

CARAMEL FLAN

Makes 10 to 12 servings

¾ **cup sugar**
4 **eggs**
1¾ **cups water**
1 **(14-ounce) can Eagle® Brand Sweetened Condensed Milk (NOT evaporated milk)**
½ **teaspoon vanilla extract**
⅛ **teaspoon salt**

Preheat oven to 350°. In heavy skillet, over medium heat, cook sugar, stirring constantly until melted and caramel-colored. Pour into ungreased 9-inch round or square baking pan, tilting to coat bottom completely. In medium bowl, beat eggs; stir in water, sweetened condensed milk, vanilla and salt. Pour over caramelized sugar; set pan in larger pan (a broiler pan). Fill pan with 1 inch hot water. Bake 55 to 60 minutes or until knife inserted near center comes out clean. Cool. Chill thoroughly. Loosen side of flan with knife; invert onto serving plate with rim. Garnish as desired. Refrigerate leftovers.

LEMON CRUNCH PARFAITS

Makes 4 to 6 servings

¼ **cup margarine or butter, melted**
2 **tablespoons light brown sugar**
½ **cup unsifted flour**
¼ **cup chopped nuts**
1 **(14-ounce) can Eagle® Brand Sweetened Condensed Milk (NOT evaporated milk)**
¼ **cup ReaLemon® Lemon Juice from Concentrate**
1 **(8-ounce) container Borden® Lite-line® Lemon Yogurt**
Few drops yellow food coloring, optional

Preheat oven to 350°. Combine margarine, sugar, flour and nuts. Spread evenly in 8-inch square baking pan. Bake 10 minutes, stirring after 5 minutes. Cool. In medium bowl, combine sweetened condensed milk and ReaLemon; stir in yogurt and food coloring if desired. In parfait or dessert glasses, layer crumbs and yogurt mixture. Chill thoroughly. Refrigerate leftovers.

LUSCIOUS LEMON CREAM

Makes about 3 cups

2 **eggs**
1 **cup sugar**
⅓ **cup ReaLemon® Lemon Juice from Concentrate**
1 **tablespoon cornstarch**
½ **cup water**
1 **teaspoon vanilla extract**
1 **cup (½ pint) Borden® Whipping Cream, whipped**

In small bowl, beat eggs, ½ *cup* sugar and ReaLemon until foamy; set aside. In medium saucepan, combine remaining ½ *cup* sugar and cornstarch. Gradually add water; mix well. Over medium heat, cook and stir until thickened and clear; remove from heat. Gradually beat in egg mixture. Over low heat, cook and stir until slightly thickened. Remove from heat; add vanilla. Cool to room temperature. Fold whipped cream into sauce. Chill. Serve with fresh fruit. Refrigerate leftovers.

Luscious Lemon Cream

FROZEN PASSION ▲

Makes 2 to 3 quarts

**2 (14-ounce) cans Eagle® Brand
  Sweetened Condensed Milk (NOT
  evaporated milk)**
**1 (2-liter) bottle *or* 2 (28-ounce) bottles
  or 5 (12-ounce) cans carbonated
  beverage, any flavor**

In ice cream freezer container, combine
ingredients; mix well. Freeze according to
manufacturer's instructions. Store leftovers in
freezer.

Passion Shakes: In blender container,
combine *one-half* can sweetened condensed
milk, *1 (12-ounce) can or 1½ cups* carbonated
beverage and *3 cups* ice. Blend until smooth.
Repeat for additional shakes. Store leftovers in
freezer. (Makes 1 or 2 quarts)

PEACHES ROMANOFF

Makes 10 to 12 servings

**1 (9-ounce) package None Such®
  Condensed Mincemeat, crumbled**
½ cup water
½ cup light rum
**1 (4-serving size) package vanilla flavor
  pudding and pie filling mix**
**1 cup (½ pint) Borden® Whipping
  Cream, whipped**
10 to 12 peach halves

In small saucepan, combine mincemeat and
water. Over medium heat, bring to a boil; cook
and stir 1 minute. Add ¼ *cup* rum. Chill.
Prepare pudding mix according to package
directions; stir in remaining ¼ *cup* rum. Cool.
Fold whipped cream into pudding. Chill. To
serve, in individual dessert dishes, spoon about
⅓ cup pudding; top with peach half, cut-side
up. Spoon 1 to 2 tablespoons mincemeat into
each peach half. Refrigerate leftovers.

RICH LEMON SAUCE

Makes about 1⅔ cups

½ cup margarine or butter
1 cup sugar
**⅓ cup ReaLemon® Lemon Juice from
  Concentrate**
3 eggs, beaten

In medium saucepan, melt margarine. Add
sugar and ReaLemon; mix well. Gradually add
eggs to ReaLemon mixture. Over low heat,
cook and stir constantly until smooth and
thick. Serve warm with ice cream, pound cake
or fruit. Refrigerate leftovers.

MICROWAVE: In 1-quart glass measure,
melt margarine on 100% power (high) 45
seconds. Add sugar and ReaLemon; mix well.
Gradually add eggs to ReaLemon mixture,
stirring briskly. Cook on 50% power (medium)
4 to 7 minutes or until thickened, stirring
briskly after each minute (*do not overheat*).

BUTTERSCOTCH APPLE DIP

Makes about 1¾ cups

1 (14-ounce) can Eagle® Brand Sweetened Condensed Milk (NOT evaporated milk)
1 cup butterscotch flavored chips
¼ teaspoon salt
2 teaspoons white vinegar
¼ to ½ teaspoon ground cinnamon
Apple wedges

In heavy saucepan, over low heat, combine sweetened condensed milk, chips and salt. Cook and stir until chips melt. Remove from heat; stir in vinegar and cinnamon. Serve warm with apples. Refrigerate leftovers.

To Reheat: In small heavy saucepan, combine desired amount of sauce with small amount of water. Over low heat, stir constantly until heated through.

Tip: Can be served warm over ice cream. Can be made several weeks ahead. Store tightly covered in refrigerator.

MICROWAVE: In 1-quart glass measure, combine sweetened condensed milk, chips and salt. Cook on 100% power (high) 3 to 3½ minutes, stirring after 2 minutes. Stir in vinegar and cinnamon.

Butterscotch Apple Dip

COCO MOCHA MOUSSE ▲

Makes 8 to 10 servings

1 envelope unflavored gelatine
¼ cup cold water
1 (15-ounce) can Coco Lopez® Cream of Coconut
¼ cup strong cold coffee *or* coffee-flavored liqueur
3 tablespoons unsweetened cocoa
2 cups (1 pint) Borden® Whipping Cream, whipped

In small saucepan, sprinkle gelatine over water; let stand 1 minute. Over low heat, stir until gelatine dissolves. In medium bowl, combine cream of coconut, coffee and cocoa; stir in gelatine mixture. Chill 10 minutes. Fold in whipped cream; spoon into individual serving dishes. Chill 1 hour or until set. Garnish as desired. Refrigerate leftovers.

COCONUT PRALINE SAUCE

Makes about 1¾ cups

¼ cup margarine or butter
1 cup Coco Lopez® Cream of Coconut
½ cup chopped pecans
½ cup flaked coconut

In small saucepan, combine ingredients. Over medium heat, bring to a boil; reduce heat and simmer uncovered 5 minutes, stirring occasionally. Serve warm over ice cream, pound cake or fruit. Refrigerate leftovers.

PUMPKIN RUM CUSTARDS

Makes 8 to 10 servings

1 cup sugar
4 eggs
1 (14-ounce) can Eagle® Brand Sweetened Condensed Milk (NOT evaporated milk)
1½ cups water
1 (16-ounce) can pumpkin (about 2 cups)
⅓ cup light rum
½ teaspoon ground nutmeg
½ teaspoon salt
⅛ to ¼ teaspoon ground ginger

Preheat oven to 350°. In heavy skillet, over medium heat, cook sugar, stirring constantly until melted and caramel-colored. Using eight to ten 6-ounce custard cups, pour about 1 tablespoon caramelized sugar on bottom of each. In large mixer bowl, beat eggs; stir in remaining ingredients. Pour equal portions of mixture into prepared cups. Set cups in shallow pan; fill pan with 1 inch hot water. Bake 50 to 60 minutes or until knife inserted in center comes out clean. Cool. Chill thoroughly. Invert custards onto serving plates. Garnish as desired. Refrigerate leftovers.

FRUITED MELBA SAUCE

Makes about 2½ cups

1 (10-ounce) package frozen red raspberries in syrup, thawed and drained, reserving syrup
1⅓ cups (one-half 28-ounce jar) None Such® Ready-to-Use Mincemeat
3 tablespoons amaretto liqueur
Toasted slivered almonds, optional

In medium saucepan, combine reserved syrup and mincemeat. Over medium heat, bring mixture to a boil; reduce heat and simmer uncovered 5 minutes, stirring occasionally. Remove from heat; stir in liqueur and raspberries. Serve warm or cold over ice cream, pound cake or peach halves; garnish with almonds if desired. Store sauce covered in refrigerator.

NEAPOLITAN PUDDING ▲

Makes 8 to 10 servings

1 (14-ounce) can Eagle® Brand Sweetened Condensed Milk (NOT evaporated milk)
1½ cups cold water
1 (4-serving size) package *instant* vanilla flavor pudding and pie filling mix
2 cups (1 pint) Borden® Whipping Cream, whipped
36 vanilla wafers
1 quart fresh strawberries, cleaned, hulled and sliced
¾ cup mini chocolate chips
Additional mini chips, vanilla wafers and strawberries, optional .

In large bowl, combine sweetened condensed milk and water. Add pudding mix; beat well. Chill 5 minutes. Fold in whipped cream. Spoon *2 cups* pudding into 3-quart glass serving bowl; top with half each of the wafers, strawberries, mini chips and remaining pudding. Repeat layering, ending with pudding. Garnish with additional mini chips, wafers and strawberries if desired. Chill thoroughly. Refrigerate leftovers.

EASY HOMEMADE CHOCOLATE ICE CREAM

Makes about 1½ quarts

1 (14-ounce) can Eagle® Brand Sweetened Condensed Milk (NOT evaporated milk)
⅔ cup chocolate flavored syrup
2 cups (1 pint) Borden® Whipping Cream, whipped (*do not use non-dairy whipped topping*)

In large bowl, combine sweetened condensed milk and syrup; mix well. Fold in whipped cream. Pour into 9×5-inch loaf pan or other 2-quart container; cover. Freeze 6 hours or until firm. Return leftovers to freezer.

French Vanilla: Omit syrup. In large bowl, combine sweetened condensed milk, 3 beaten egg yolks* and 4 teaspoons vanilla; mix well. Fold in whipped cream.

Peppermint Candy: Omit syrup. In large bowl, combine sweetened condensed milk, 3 beaten egg yolks* and 4 teaspoons vanilla; mix well. Fold in whipped cream and ¼ to ½ cup crushed hard peppermint candy.

Buttered Pecan: Omit syrup. Combine 2 tablespoons melted butter and ½ to ¾ cup chopped pecans. In large bowl, combine sweetened condensed milk, 3 beaten egg yolks,* 1 teaspoon maple flavoring and buttered pecans; mix well. Fold in whipped cream.

Mint Chocolate Chip: Omit syrup. In large bowl, combine sweetened condensed milk, 3 beaten egg yolks,* 2 teaspoons peppermint extract and 3 to 4 drops green food coloring if desired; mix well. Fold in whipped cream and ½ cup mini chocolate chips.

Coffee: Omit syrup. In large bowl, combine sweetened condensed milk, 1 tablespoon instant coffee dissolved in 1 teaspoon hot water, 3 beaten egg yolks* and 4 teaspoons vanilla; mix well. Fold in whipped cream.

Strawberry: Omit syrup. In blender, blend 1 (10-ounce) package thawed frozen strawberries in syrup until smooth. In large bowl, combine pureed strawberries, sweetened condensed milk, 3 beaten egg yolks,* 1½ teaspoons vanilla and few drops red food coloring if desired; mix well. Fold in whipped cream.

*Use only Grade A clean, uncracked eggs.

COOKIES
& CANDIES

Try make-in-one-pan Magic Cookie Bars—nothing's easier! Drop cookies, bar cookies, molded cookies, fun-to-make cut-out cookies— choose your favorite and bake a batch! Don't wait for a holiday to make Foolproof Fudge—always rich, smooth and creamy! The kids can make the easy cookies and candies featured here.

◄VERSATILE CUT-OUT COOKIES

Makes about 6½ dozen

3⅓ cups unsifted flour
  1 tablespoon baking powder
  ½ teaspoon salt
  1 (14-ounce) can Eagle® Brand Sweetened Condensed Milk (NOT evaporated milk)
  ¾ cup margarine or butter, softened
  2 eggs
  2 teaspoons vanilla *or* 1½ teaspoons almond *or* lemon extract
  Ready-to-spread frosting

Preheat oven to 350°. Combine flour, baking powder and salt; set aside. In large bowl, beat sweetened condensed milk, margarine, eggs and vanilla until well blended. Add dry ingredients; mix well. Chill 2 hours. On floured surface, lightly knead dough to form a smooth ball. Divide into thirds. On well-floured surface, roll out each portion to ⅛-inch thickness. Cut with floured cookie cutter. Place 1 inch apart on greased baking sheets. Bake 7 to 9 minutes or until lightly browned around edges. Cool thoroughly. Frost with ready-to-spread frosting and decorate as desired. Store loosely covered at room temperature.

Sandwich Cookies: Use 2½-inch cookie cutter. Bake as directed. Sandwich 2 cookies together with ready-to-spread frosting. Sprinkle with sugar if desired. (Makes about 3 dozen)

FUDGY BROWNIES WITH A CRUST

Makes 36 bars

1¾ cups unsifted flour
  ¼ cup sugar
  ½ cup plus 2 tablespoons cold margarine or butter
  1 (12-ounce) package semi-sweet chocolate chips
  1 (14-ounce) can Eagle® Brand Sweetened Condensed Milk (NOT evaporated milk)
  ¾ cup chopped nuts
  1 teaspoon vanilla extract
  ½ teaspoon baking powder
  Confectioners' sugar

Preheat oven to 350°. In medium bowl, combine *1 cup* flour and sugar. Cut in *½ cup* margarine until mixture resembles coarse corn meal. Press firmly on bottom of ungreased 13×9-inch baking pan. Bake 15 minutes. Meanwhile, in heavy saucepan, over low heat, melt chips and remaining *2 tablespoons* margarine with sweetened condensed milk. Remove from heat; stir in remaining *¾ cup* flour, nuts, vanilla and baking powder. Spread evenly over prepared crust. Bake 20 to 25 minutes or until center is set. Cool. Sprinkle with confectioners' sugar. Cut into bars. Store tightly covered at room temperature.

MINCE OATMEAL COOKIES

Makes about 5 dozen

3 cups quick-cooking oats
1½ cups firmly packed light brown sugar
1½ cups unsifted flour
1 teaspoon baking soda
½ teaspoon salt
½ cup vegetable oil
3 eggs, beaten
3 tablespoons water
1 (9-ounce) package None Such®
  Condensed Mincemeat, crumbled

Preheat oven to 350°. In large bowl, stir together dry ingredients. Add oil, eggs and water. Stir in mincemeat. Drop by rounded teaspoonfuls 2 inches apart onto well-greased baking sheets. Bake 8 to 10 minutes or until lightly browned. Immediately remove from baking sheets.

FRUIT & NUT SNACK BARS

Makes 24 to 36 bars

½ cup margarine or butter, softened
1¼ cups granulated sugar
3 eggs
1⅓ cups (one-half 28-ounce jar) None
  Such® Ready-to-Use Mincemeat
  (Regular *or* Brandy & Rum)
½ cup chopped pecans
2 (1-ounce) squares unsweetened
  chocolate, melted
¼ teaspoon salt
1½ cups unsifted flour
  Confectioners' sugar
  Pecan halves, optional

Preheat oven to 350°. In large mixer bowl, beat margarine and granulated sugar until fluffy. Add eggs; beat well. Stir in mincemeat, chopped pecans, chocolate and salt; mix well. Stir in flour. Spread evenly into lightly greased 13×9-inch baking pan. Bake 30 minutes or until wooden pick inserted near center comes out clean. Cool. Sprinkle with confectioners' sugar. Cut into bars. Garnish with pecan halves if desired.

CRUMBLY-TOPPED LEMON MINCE BARS

Makes 24 to 36 bars

1¼ cups unsifted flour
1 cup firmly packed light brown sugar
1 cup flaked coconut
1 cup finely crushed saltines (about 28)
½ cup margarine or butter, melted
2 teaspoons grated lemon rind
½ teaspoon baking soda
1⅓ cups (one-half 28-ounce jar) None
  Such® Ready-to-Use Mincemeat
½ cup chopped nuts, optional

Preheat oven to 350°. In large bowl, combine all ingredients except mincemeat and nuts; blend well. Reserving *1 cup* crumb mixture, press remainder firmly on bottom of 13×9-inch baking dish. Spoon mincemeat over crust; top with reserved crumbs and nuts if desired. Press down gently. Bake 30 minutes or until edges are lightly browned. Cool completely; cut into bars.

Left to Right: Mince Oatmeal Cookies, Fruit & Nut Snack Bars, Crumbly-Topped Lemon Mince Bars, Chocolate Fruit Truffles, Chocolate Spice Cookies

CHOCOLATE FRUIT TRUFFLES

Makes about 6 dozen

2½ cups vanilla wafer crumbs (about 65 wafers)
1 (14-ounce) can Eagle® Brand Sweetened Condensed Milk (NOT evaporated milk)
1 (9-ounce) package None Such® Condensed Mincemeat, crumbled
1 cup chopped cashews *or* almonds
½ cup chopped candied cherries
2 tablespoons unsweetened cocoa
½ teaspoon almond extract
   Confectioners' sugar
   Additional candied cherries, optional

In large bowl, combine all ingredients except confectioners' sugar and additional candied cherries until well blended. Chill 4 hours or overnight. Dip hands in confectioners' sugar; shape mixture into 1-inch balls. (Rechill if mixture becomes too soft.) Roll in confectioners' sugar. Place on wax paper-lined baking sheets; chill 2 hours or until firm. Store tightly covered in refrigerator. Garnish with additional candied cherries if desired.

Tip: Flavor of these candies improves after 24 hours. They can be made ahead and stored in refrigerator for several weeks.

CHOCOLATE SPICE COOKIES

Makes about 4 dozen

2 cups unsifted flour
½ cup unsweetened cocoa
1 teaspoon baking soda
½ teaspoon salt
1¼ cups sugar
¾ cup shortening
¼ cup margarine or butter, softened
2 eggs
2 teaspoons vanilla extract
1 (9-ounce) package None Such® Condensed Mincemeat, crumbled
1 cup chopped nuts, optional

Preheat oven to 350°. Stir together flour, cocoa, baking soda and salt; set aside. In large mixer bowl, beat sugar, shortening and margarine until fluffy. Beat in eggs and vanilla. Add flour mixture; mix well. Stir in mincemeat and nuts if desired. Roll into 1¼-inch balls; place 2 inches apart on ungreased baking sheets. Flatten slightly. Bake 8 to 10 minutes or until almost no imprint remains when lightly touched *(do not overbake)*.

Clockwise from Bottom: Peanut Butter Logs, Layered Mint Chocolate Candy, Creamy White Cherry Fudge, Coconut Rum Balls, Chocolate Pecan Critters

In heavy saucepan, over low heat, melt chips with sweetened condensed milk. Add marshmallows; stir until melted. Remove from heat; cool 20 minutes. Divide in half; place each portion on a 20-inch piece of wax paper. Shape each into 12-inch log. Roll in nuts. Wrap tightly; chill 2 hours or until firm. Remove paper; cut into ¼-inch slices.

MICROWAVE: In 2-quart glass measure, cook chips, sweetened condensed milk and marshmallows on 100% power (high) 4 minutes or until melted, stirring after 2 minutes. Let stand at room temperature 1 hour. Proceed as above.

Peanut Butter Fudge: Stir peanuts into mixture. Spread into wax paper-lined 8- or 9-inch square pan. Chill 2 hours or until firm. Turn fudge onto cutting board; peel off paper and cut into squares.

CHOCOLATE PECAN CRITTERS

Makes about 5 dozen

1 (11½-ounce) package milk chocolate chips
1 (6-ounce) package semi-sweet chocolate chips
¼ cup margarine or butter
1 (14-ounce) can Eagle® Brand Sweetened Condensed Milk (NOT evaporated milk)
⅛ teaspoon salt
2 cups coarsely chopped pecans
2 teaspoons vanilla extract
    Pecan halves

In heavy saucepan, over medium heat, melt chips and margarine with sweetened condensed milk and salt. Remove from heat; stir in chopped nuts and vanilla. Drop by teaspoonfuls onto wax paper-lined baking sheets. Top with pecan halves. Chill. Store tightly covered.

MICROWAVE: In 2-quart glass measure, cook chips, margarine, sweetened condensed milk and salt on 100% power (high) 3 minutes, stirring after 1½ minutes. Stir to melt chips; stir in chopped nuts and vanilla. Proceed as above.

PEANUT BUTTER LOGS

Makes two 12-inch logs

1 (12-ounce) package peanut butter flavored chips
1 (14-ounce) can Eagle® Brand Sweetened Condensed Milk (NOT evaporated milk)
1 cup Campfire® Miniature Marshmallows
1 cup chopped peanuts

CREAMY WHITE CHERRY FUDGE

Makes about 2¼ pounds

1½ pounds white confectioners' coating*
1 (14-ounce) can Eagle® Brand Sweetened Condensed Milk (NOT evaporated milk)
⅛ teaspoon salt
1 cup chopped candied cherries
1½ teaspoons vanilla extract

In heavy saucepan, over low heat, melt coating with sweetened condensed milk and salt. Remove from heat; stir in cherries and vanilla. Spread evenly into wax paper-lined 8- or 9-inch square pan. Chill 2 hours or until firm. Turn fudge onto cutting board; peel off paper and cut into squares. Store tightly covered at room temperature.

MICROWAVE: In 2-quart glass measure, combine coating, sweetened condensed milk and salt. Cook on 100% power (high) 3 to 5 minutes or until coating melts, stirring after 3 minutes. Stir in vanilla and cherries. Proceed as above.

*White confectioners' coating can be purchased in candy specialty stores.

PRIZE COOKIES

Makes about 6½ dozen

1 cup shortening
1½ cups sugar
3 eggs
3 cups unsifted flour
1 teaspoon baking soda
½ teaspoon salt
1⅓ cups (one-half 28-ounce jar) None Such® Ready-to-Use Mincemeat (Regular or Brandy & Rum)

Preheat oven to 375°. In large mixer bowl, beat shortening and sugar until fluffy. Add eggs; beat well. Stir together dry ingredients; gradually add to shortening mixture. Mix well. Stir in mincemeat. Drop by rounded teaspoonfuls, 2 inches apart, onto greased baking sheets. Bake 8 to 10 minutes or until lightly browned. Cool. Frost if desired.

Tip: For a more chewy cookie, substitute 1 (9-ounce) package None Such® Condensed Mincemeat for Ready-to-Use Mincemeat.

LAYERED MINT CHOCOLATE CANDY

Makes about 1¾ pounds

1 (12-ounce) package semi-sweet chocolate chips
1 (14-ounce) can Eagle® Brand Sweetened Condensed Milk (NOT evaporated milk)
2 teaspoons vanilla extract
6 ounces white confectioners' coating
1 tablespoon peppermint extract
Few drops green or red food coloring, optional

In heavy saucepan, over low heat, melt chips with *1 cup* sweetened condensed milk. Stir in vanilla. Spread half the mixture into wax paper-lined 8- or 9-inch square pan; chill 10 minutes or until firm. Hold remaining chocolate mixture at room temperature. In heavy saucepan, over low heat, melt coating with remaining sweetened condensed milk. Stir in peppermint extract and food coloring if desired. Spread on chilled chocolate layer; chill 10 minutes longer or until firm. Spread reserved chocolate mixture on mint layer. Chill 2 hours or until firm. Turn onto cutting board; peel off paper and cut into squares. Store loosely covered at room temperature.

COCONUT RUM BALLS

Makes about 8 dozen

1 (12-ounce) package vanilla wafer cookies, finely crushed (about 3 cups crumbs)
1 (3½-ounce) can flaked coconut (1⅓ cups)
1 cup finely chopped nuts
1 (14-ounce) can Eagle® Brand Sweetened Condensed Milk (NOT evaporated milk)
¼ cup rum
Additional flaked coconut

In large bowl, combine crumbs, coconut and nuts. Add sweetened condensed milk and rum; mix well. Chill 4 hours. Shape into 1-inch balls. Roll in coconut. Store tightly covered in refrigerator.

Tip: Flavor of these candies improves after 24 hours. They can be made ahead and stored in refrigerator for several weeks.

PUMPKIN CHEESECAKE BARS ▲

Makes 48 bars

1 (16-ounce) package pound cake mix
3 eggs
2 tablespoons margarine or butter, melted
4 teaspoons pumpkin pie spice
1 (8-ounce) package cream cheese, softened
1 (14-ounce) can Eagle® Brand Sweetened Condensed Milk (NOT evaporated milk)
1 (16-ounce) can pumpkin (about 2 cups)
½ teaspoon salt
1 cup chopped nuts

Preheat oven to 350°. In large mixer bowl, on low speed, combine cake mix, *1 egg*, margarine and *2 teaspoons* pumpkin pie spice until crumbly. Press onto bottom of 15×10-inch jellyroll pan. In large mixer bowl, beat cheese until fluffy. Gradually beat in sweetened condensed milk then remaining *2 eggs*, pumpkin, remaining *2 teaspoons* pumpkin pie spice and salt; mix well. Pour over crust; sprinkle with nuts. Bake 30 to 35 minutes or until set. Cool. Chill; cut into bars. Store covered in refrigerator.

CRUNCHY CLUSTERS

Makes about 3 dozen

1 (12-ounce) package semi-sweet chocolate chips *or* 3 (6-ounce) packages butterscotch flavored chips
1 (14-ounce) can Eagle® Brand Sweetened Condensed Milk (NOT evaporated milk)
1 (3-ounce) can chow mein noodles *or* 2 cups pretzel sticks, broken into ½-inch pieces
1 cup dry roasted peanuts *or* whole roasted almonds

In heavy saucepan, over low heat, melt chips with sweetened condensed milk. Remove from heat. In large bowl, combine noodles and nuts; stir in chocolate mixture. Drop by tablespoonfuls onto wax paper-lined baking sheets; chill 2 hours or until firm. Store loosely covered at room temperature.

MICROWAVE: In 2-quart glass measure, combine chips and sweetened condensed milk. Cook on 100% power (high) 3 minutes, stirring after 1½ minutes. Stir until smooth. Proceed as above.

PECAN PIE BARS ▶

Makes 36 bars

2 cups unsifted flour
½ cup confectioners' sugar
1 cup cold margarine or butter
1 (14-ounce) can Eagle® Brand
   Sweetened Condensed Milk (NOT
   evaporated milk)
1 egg
1 teaspoon vanilla extract
1 (6-ounce) package almond brickle
   chips
1 cup chopped pecans

Preheat oven to 350° (325° for glass dish). In medium bowl, combine flour and sugar; cut in margarine until crumbly. Press firmly on bottom of 13×9-inch baking pan. Bake 15 minutes. Meanwhile, in medium bowl, beat sweetened condensed milk, egg and vanilla. Stir in chips and pecans. Spread evenly over crust. Bake 25 minutes or until golden brown. Cool. Cut into bars. Store covered in refrigerator.

CHOCOLATE 'N' OAT BARS

Makes 36 bars

1 cup unsifted flour
1 cup quick-cooking oats
¾ cup firmly packed light brown sugar
½ cup margarine or butter, softened
1 (14-ounce) can Eagle® Brand
   Sweetened Condensed Milk (NOT
   evaporated milk)
1 cup chopped nuts
1 (6-ounce) package semi-sweet
   chocolate chips

Preheat oven to 350° (325° for glass dish). In large bowl, combine flour, oats, sugar and margarine; mix well. Reserving ½ cup oat mixture, press remainder on bottom of 13×9-inch baking pan. Bake 10 minutes. Pour sweetened condensed milk evenly over crust. Sprinkle with nuts and chocolate chips. Top with remaining oat mixture; press down firmly. Bake 25 to 30 minutes or until lightly browned. Cool. Store covered at room temperature.

FRUITED SHORTBREAD COOKIES

Makes about 3 dozen

2½ cups unsifted flour
1 teaspoon baking soda
1 teaspoon cream of tartar
1 cup margarine or butter, softened
1½ cups confectioners' sugar
1 egg
1 (9-ounce) package None Such®
   Condensed Mincemeat, crumbled
1 teaspoon vanilla extract
   Lemon Frosting, optional
   Candied cherries or nuts, optional

Preheat oven to 375°. Stir together flour, baking soda and cream of tartar; set aside. In large mixer bowl, beat margarine and sugar until fluffy. Add egg; mix well. Stir in mincemeat and vanilla. Add flour mixture; mix well (dough will be stiff). Roll into 1¼-inch balls. Place on ungreased baking sheets; flatten slightly. Bake 10 to 12 minutes or until lightly browned. Cool. Frost with Lemon Frosting and garnish with candied cherries or nuts if desired.

Lemon Frosting: In small mixer bowl, beat 2 cups confectioners' sugar, 2 tablespoons softened margarine or butter, 2 tablespoons water and ½ teaspoon grated lemon rind until well blended. (Makes about ⅔ cup)

Foolproof Dark Chocolate Fudge (top), Strawberry Bon Bons (bottom)

FOOLPROOF DARK CHOCOLATE FUDGE

Makes about 2 pounds

3 (6-ounce) packages semi-sweet chocolate chips
1 (14-ounce) can Eagle® Brand Sweetened Condensed Milk (NOT evaporated milk)
Dash salt
½ to 1 cup chopped nuts
1½ teaspoons vanilla extract

In heavy saucepan, over low heat, melt chips with sweetened condensed milk and salt. Remove from heat; stir in nuts and vanilla. Spread evenly into wax paper-lined 8- or 9-inch square pan. Chill 2 hours or until firm. Turn fudge onto cutting board; peel off paper and cut into squares. Store loosely covered at room temperature.

MICROWAVE: In 1-quart glass measure, combine chips with sweetened condensed milk. Cook on 100% power (high) 2½ to 3 minutes. Stir until chips melt and mixture is smooth. Add remaining ingredients. Proceed as above.

Creamy Dark Chocolate Fudge: Melt 2 cups Campfire® Miniature Marshmallows with chips and sweetened condensed milk. Proceed as above.

Milk Chocolate Fudge: Omit 1 (6-ounce) package semi-sweet chocolate chips. Add 1 cup milk chocolate chips. Proceed as above.

Creamy Milk Chocolate Fudge: Omit 1 (6-ounce) package semi-sweet chocolate chips. Add 1 cup milk chocolate chips and 2 cups Campfire® Miniature Marshmallows. Proceed as above.

Mexican Chocolate Fudge: Reduce vanilla to 1 teaspoon. Add 1 tablespoon instant coffee and 1 teaspoon ground cinnamon to sweetened condensed milk. Proceed as above.

Butterscotch Fudge: Omit chocolate chips and vanilla. In heavy saucepan, melt 2 (12-ounce) packages butterscotch flavored chips with sweetened condensed milk. Remove from heat; stir in 2 tablespoons white vinegar, ⅛ teaspoon salt, ½ teaspoon maple flavoring and 1 cup chopped nuts. Proceed as above.

STRAWBERRY BON BONS

Makes about 60 candies

1 (14-ounce) can Eagle® Brand
    Sweetened Condensed Milk (NOT
    evaporated milk)
2 (7-ounce) packages flaked coconut
    (5⅓ cups)
1 (8-serving size) package strawberry
    flavor gelatin
1 cup ground blanched almonds
1 teaspoon almond extract
    Red food coloring
2¼ cups sifted confectioners' sugar
3 tablespoons Borden® Whipping
    Cream
    Green food coloring

In large bowl, combine sweetened condensed milk, coconut, ⅓ cup gelatin, almonds, extract and enough red food coloring to tint mixture a strawberry shade. Chill 1 hour or until firm enough to handle. Using about ½ tablespoon for each, form into strawberry shapes. Sprinkle remaining gelatin onto wax paper; roll each strawberry in gelatin to coat. Place on wax paper-lined baking sheets; chill. In small bowl, combine sugar, cream and green food coloring. Using pastry bag with open star tip, pipe small amount on top each strawberry. Store covered at room temperature or in refrigerator.

Tip: Green tube decorator icing can be used to make strawberry "stems." Omit confectioners' sugar, cream and green food coloring.

DOUBLE PEANUT GRANOLA SNACK

Makes about 6½ cups

½ cup peanut butter
¼ cup honey
¼ cup firmly packed brown sugar
2 tablespoons vegetable oil
1 (9-ounce) package None Such®
    Condensed Mincemeat, crumbled
2 cups quick-cooking oats
1 cup salted peanuts

Preheat oven to 250°. In large saucepan, stir together peanut butter, honey, sugar and oil; add mincemeat. Over medium heat, bring to a boil; cook and stir 1 minute. Remove from heat. Add oats and peanuts; mix well. Spoon into 13×9-inch aluminum foil-lined baking pan. Bake 45 minutes, stirring every 15 minutes. Cool. Break into chunks. Store in tightly covered container.

Tip: To freshen Granola Snack, place on baking sheet and bake at 250° for 10 minutes. Cool.

LEMON BLOSSOM COOKIES

Makes about 6 dozen

2 cups margarine or butter, softened
1½ cups confectioners' sugar
¼ cup ReaLemon® Lemon Juice from
    Concentrate
4 cups unsifted flour
    Finely chopped nuts, optional
    Assorted Bama® Fruit Preserves and
    Jams *or* pecan halves

Preheat oven to 350°. In large mixer bowl, beat margarine and sugar until fluffy. Add ReaLemon; beat well. Gradually add flour; mix well. Chill 2 hours. Shape into 1-inch balls; roll in nuts if desired. Place 1 inch apart on greased baking sheets. Press thumb in center of each ball; fill with preserves or pecan halves. Bake 14 to 16 minutes or until lightly browned.

Lemon Blossom Cookies

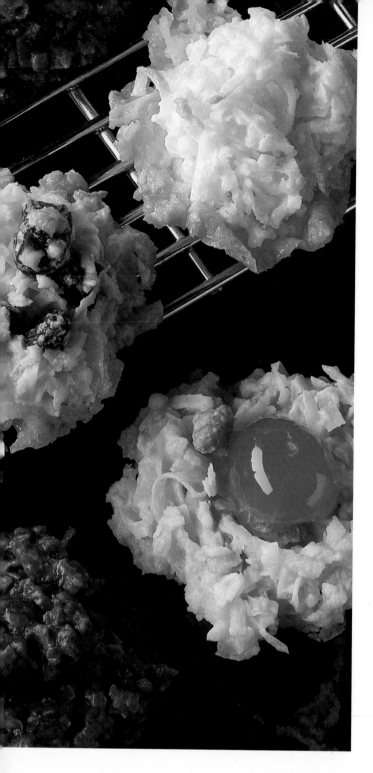

Preheat oven to 350°. In large bowl, combine coconut, sweetened condensed milk and extracts; mix well. Drop by rounded teaspoonfuls onto aluminum foil-lined and *generously greased* baking sheets; garnish as desired. Bake 8 to 10 minutes or until lightly browned around edges. *Immediately* remove from baking sheets (macaroons will stick if allowed to cool). Store loosely covered at room temperature.

Chocolate: Omit almond extract. Add 4 (1-ounce) squares unsweetened chocolate, melted. Proceed as above.

Chocolate Chip: Omit almond extract. Add 1 cup mini chocolate chips. Proceed as above.

Cherry Nut: Omit almond extract. Add 1 cup chopped nuts and 2 tablespoons maraschino cherry syrup. Press maraschino cherry half into center of each macaroon before baking.

Rum Raisin: Omit almond extract. Add 1 cup raisins and 1 teaspoon rum flavoring. Proceed as above.

EASY PEANUT BUTTER COOKIES

Makes about 5 dozen

> 1 (14-ounce) can Eagle® Brand Sweetened Condensed Milk (NOT evaporated milk)
> ¾ cup peanut butter
> 2 cups biscuit baking mix
> 1 teaspoon vanilla extract
> Granulated sugar

Preheat oven to 375°. In large mixer bowl, beat sweetened condensed milk and peanut butter until smooth. Add biscuit mix and vanilla; mix well. Shape into 1-inch balls. Roll in sugar. Place 2 inches apart on ungreased baking sheets. Flatten with fork. Bake 6 to 8 minutes or until *lightly* browned (*do not overbake*). Cool. Store tightly covered at room temperature.

Peanut Blossoms: Shape as above; *do not flatten*. Bake as above. Press solid milk chocolate candy drop in center of each ball immediately after baking.

Peanut Butter & Jelly Gems: Press thumb in center of each ball of dough; fill with jelly, jam or preserves. Bake as above.

COCONUT MACAROONS ▲

Makes about 4 dozen

> 2 (7-ounce) packages *flaked* coconut (5⅓ cups)
> 1 (14-ounce) can Eagle® Brand Sweetened Condensed Milk (NOT evaporated milk)
> 2 teaspoons vanilla extract
> 1½ teaspoons almond extract

Magic Peanut Cookie Bars

MAGIC COOKIE BARS

Makes 24 to 36 bars

- ½ cup margarine or butter
- 1½ cups graham cracker crumbs
- 1 (14-ounce) can Eagle® Brand Sweetened Condensed Milk (NOT evaporated milk)
- 1 (6-ounce) package semi-sweet chocolate chips
- 1 (3½-ounce) can flaked coconut (1⅓ cups)
- 1 cup chopped nuts

Preheat oven to 350° (325° for glass dish). In 13×9-inch baking pan, melt margarine in oven. Sprinkle crumbs over margarine; pour sweetened condensed milk evenly over crumbs. Top with remaining ingredients; press down firmly. Bake 25 to 30 minutes or until lightly browned. Cool. Chill if desired. Cut into bars. Store loosely covered at room temperature.

Seven Layer Magic Cookie Bars: Add 1 (6-ounce) package butterscotch flavored chips after chocolate chips.

Magic Peanut Cookie Bars: Omit chocolate chips and nuts. Substitute 2 cups chocolate-covered peanuts (about ¾ pound).

RICH LEMON BARS

Makes 30 bars

- 1½ cups plus 3 tablespoons unsifted flour
- ½ cup confectioners' sugar
- ¾ cup cold margarine or butter
- 4 eggs, slightly beaten
- 1½ cups granulated sugar
- 1 teaspoon baking powder
- ½ cup ReaLemon® Lemon Juice from Concentrate
  Additional confectioners' sugar

Preheat oven to 350°. In medium bowl, combine *1½ cups* flour and confectioners' sugar; cut in margarine until crumbly. Press onto bottom of lightly greased 13×9-inch baking pan; bake 15 minutes. Meanwhile, in large bowl, combine eggs, granulated sugar, baking powder, ReaLemon and remaining *3 tablespoons* flour; mix well. Pour over baked crust; bake 20 to 25 minutes or until golden brown. Cool. Cut into bars. Sprinkle with additional confectioners' sugar. Store covered in refrigerator; serve at room temperature.

Lemon Pecan Bars: Omit 3 tablespoons flour in lemon mixture. Sprinkle ¾ cup finely chopped pecans over top of lemon mixture. Bake as above.

Coconut Lemon Bars: Omit 3 tablespoons flour in lemon mixture. Sprinkle ¾ cup flaked coconut over top of lemon mixture. Bake as above.

Coconut Lemon Bars

INDEX